T/

SECTION 1 THE

SECTION 2 STATE LAWS AND RULES OF THE ROAD

SECTION 3 BE IN SHAPE TO DRIVE

SECTION 4 BEFORE YOU DRIVE

SECTION 5 BASIC DRIVING

SECTION 11 SPECIAL DRIVING SITUATIONS

SECTION 12 TEST YOUR KNOWLEDGE

Section 1

The Driver's License

About This Manual

Driving is one of the most risky activities you may choose to do during your lifetime. This manual is your guide to good driving. It explains the rules of the road and what the law expects of you when operating a vehicle. Its purpose is to help you learn traffic control devices, signs, pavement markings, and proper behavior, which you must know before driving on the highway.

Types of Driver's Licenses and Driver's Permits

South Carolina (SC) issues licenses as proof that you passed an examination and are qualified to operate a particular type of vehicle. The gross vehicle weight rating (GVWR) or gross vehicle weight (GVW) determines which class of license you will need.

Non-Commercial Licenses

- **Class D:** Allows you to drive non-commercial passenger vehicles, such as cars and trucks, which do not exceed 26,000 pounds GVW. With a Class D driver's license, you may also operate a moped or three-wheel vehicle (excluding a two-wheel motorcycle with a detachable sidecar).

- **Class E:** Allows you to operate non-commercial, single unit vehicles that exceed 26,000 pounds GVW. Examples of Class E vehicles include trucks and motor homes. With a Class E driver's license, you may also operate a moped or three-wheel vehicle (excluding a two-wheel motorcycle with a detachable sidecar). Reference *SC's Large Non-Commercial and Recreational Vehicles Driver's Manual* for specific information to get this type of license.

- **Class F:** Allows you to drive non-commercial, combination vehicles that exceed 26,000 pounds GVW. Examples of Class F vehicles include trucks and motor homes with a towed trailer or vehicle. With a Class F driver's license, you may also operate a moped or three-wheel vehicle (excluding a two-wheel motorcycle with a detachable sidecar). Reference *SC's Large Non-Commercial and Recreational Vehicles Driver's Manual* for specific information to get this type of license.

- **Class G:** Allows you to operate a moped. If you have a valid driver's license or permit in any of the other four classifications, you are not required to obtain a license to drive a moped. (Minimum age 15). You are only required to pass the vision and knowledge test to get a moped license. Reference *SC's Motorcycle and Moped Operator's Manual* for specific information to get this type of license.

- **Class M:** Allows you to operate a two-wheel motorcycle, a two-wheel motorcycle with a detachable sidecar, or a three-wheel vehicle.

Reference *SC's Motorcycle and Moped Operator's Manual* for specific information to get this type of license.

Commercial Driver's Licenses (CDLs)

- **Class A:** Any combination of vehicles with a GCWR of 26,001 or more pounds provided the GVWR of the vehicle being towed is in excess of 10,000 pounds.

- **Class B:** Any single vehicle with a GVWR of 26,001 or more pounds, or any such vehicle towing a vehicle not in excess of 10,000 pounds GVWR.

- **Class C:** Any single vehicle or combination of vehicles that does not meet the definitions of Class A or B, but is designed to transport 16 or more passengers, including the driver, or is placarded for hazardous materials.

Reference SC's *Commercial Driver License Manual* for specific information to get a Class A, B, or C license.

Each qualified driver will have only one driver's license, endorsed for one or more of the classifications. It is illegal to have more than one valid driver's license. If you drive a motorcycle and another type of vehicle, your license should be endorsed for two classifications after your completion of driving tests for both types of vehicles.

When driving you must have a valid driver's license, vehicle registration, and valid insurance card in your possession for the class of vehicle you are operating. If you do not, you will be subject to a fine.

Licensing Requirements

Documentation

United States Citizens

If you are a US citizen applying for a first-time beginner's permit, driver's license, or identification card, you must provide to any branch office original documents showing proof of your US citizenship, identity, date and place of birth, social security number, and SC address. Reference the US Citizen's Checklist (SCDMV form MV-93) for a complete list of required documents.

International Customers

If you are not a US citizen, you may apply for an SC beginner's permit, driver's license, or identification card at one of the branch offices that processes applications for international customers. Reference the International Customers' Checklist (SCDMV form MV-94) for a complete list of required documents. Forms can be found on SCDMV's website at www.scdmvonline.com

Beginner's Permit

If you have never had a driver's license, you must start with a beginner's permit.

- You must be at least 15 years old.
- You must pass the vision and knowledge test.
- You may drive from 6 a.m. to midnight if a licensed driver who is at least 21 years old and has at least one year of driving experience is in the front seat with you.
- You may drive after midnight but any licensed individual listed in SC Code Section 56-1-100(A) (1-7) must supervise you.
- You must hold your beginner's permit for at least 180 days, regardless of your age, before you

may apply for any type of license. You may apply on the 181st day or anytime thereafter.

First-Time Driver's License

If you are 17 or older and applying for your first driver's license you must hold a beginner's permit for more than 180 days before attempting to take the skills test for full driving privileges.

If you are 15 or 16 and applying for your first driver's license, all of the following must be true:

- You have held your beginner's permit for more than 180 days.
- You completed a driver's education course (eight hours in the classroom and six hours driving).
- You are enrolled in school (not suspended or expelled), and you have satisfactory school attendance.
- You have practiced driving for at least 40 hours, including ten hours of night driving with one of the individuals listed below:
  1) Your father
  2) Your mother
  3) Your legal guardian
  4) An individual who has custody, care, and control of you
  5) A person with written approval by the Department of Social Services. **You must provide SCDMV with a copy of approval.**
  6) A person who has been standing in loco parentis (place of a parent) for a continuous period of not less than sixty days.

[handwritten annotation: ONLY (NOT) BRI or any friends]

7) A responsible adult who is willing to assume the obligation imposed under SC Code Section 56-1-110 and who has written permission, from a person listed in items 1 – 6 above, signed and verified before a person authorized to administer oaths (notary). **You must provide SCDMV with a copy of the notarized permission.**

- You must complete the Certification of School Attendance, Driver's Education and Driving Practice (SCDMV form PDLA). You will receive the PDLA form from your driver's education program once you successfully complete the course.

Graduated Driver's License Program

[handwritten: Also known is your restricted]

The graduated driver's license program is for individuals 15 to 17 years of age. It allows you the opportunity to develop your driving skills. It restricts nighttime and unsupervised driving at first, but these restrictions are lifted over time.

Conditional License for a 15-year-old

If you are at least 15 ½, but less than 16, **and** have met the requirements listed in this section (documentation, beginner's permit, and PDLA form), you are eligible for a conditional license. You must pass the vision and skills test to receive this license. You will earn full driving privileges once you have held your conditional license for one year with no traffic offenses and have not been at-fault in any collisions.

These are the nighttime and unsupervised driving restrictions of a conditional license.

- You cannot have more than two passengers under 21 in the vehicle with you unless you are with a licensed adult who is at least 21. The **only** exception is if you are transporting family members or students to and from school.

- You may drive alone from 6 a.m. to 6 p.m. (8 p.m. during daylight savings time).
- You may drive with a licensed driver, who is at least 21, from 6 p.m. (8 p.m. during daylight savings time) to midnight.
- You may drive after midnight to 6 a.m. but you **must be supervised** by any licensed individual listed in SC Code Section 56-1-100(A) (1-7).

If you are under 17 and receive six or more points on your record before you have held your license for one year, your license will be suspended for six months.

If you are 16 and the time limitations of this license cause problems for you at your job, school, vocational training, church–sponsored activity, or parentally approved sports activity, you may apply for a special restricted license **with a waiver** to drive alone until midnight.

Special Restricted License for a 16-year-old

If you are 16, but less than 17, have met the requirements listed in this section (documentation, beginner's permit, and PDLA form), and have passed your vision and skills test, **or** if you are 16 and have a conditional license, you are eligible for a special restricted license.

These are the nighttime and unsupervised driving restrictions of a special restricted license.

- You cannot have more than two passengers under 21 in the vehicle with you unless you are with a licensed adult who is at least 21. The **only** exception is if you are transporting family members or students to and from school.

- You may drive alone from 6 a.m. to 6 p.m. (8 p.m. during daylight savings time).
- You may drive with a licensed driver, who is at least 21, from 6 p.m. (8 p.m. during daylight savings time) to midnight.
- You may drive after midnight to 6 a.m. but you **must be supervised** by any licensed individual listed in SC Code Section 56-1-100(A)(1-7).

If you are under 17 and receive six or more points on your record before you have held your license for one year, your license will be suspended for six months.

If you are 16 and the time limitations of this license cause problems for you at your job, school, vocational training, church–sponsored activity or parentally approved sports activity, you may apply for a waiver to drive alone until midnight.

Special Restricted License with a Waiver for a 16-year-old

If you are 16 and have a special restricted or conditional license, you may be eligible for a special restricted license with a waiver. The special restricted license with a waiver allows you to drive by yourself until **midnight** if you work or participate in certain extracurricular activities. The waiver will not allow you to drive after midnight.

To get a special restricted license with a waiver, you must visit an SCDMV branch and do **all** of the following:

- Complete the Application for a Beginner's Permit, Driver's License, or Identification Card (SCDMV Form 447-NC)

- Bring a letter from your school, church, work, or extracurricular activity that says why you need this waiver
- Bring a letter from your parent or legal guardian that says your parent or legal guardian is allowing you to have the waiver and why you need this waiver
- Pass the vision test
- Pay $25 for a new license that has the waiver added to it

Regular Driver's License

You will earn full driving privileges at 17, or after keeping your conditional or special restricted license for one year, if you received no traffic offenses and were not at-fault in any collisions. You do not have to visit an SCDMV branch to receive full driving privileges. You will receive a sleeve in the mail from the SCDMV that is to be wrapped around your license. You must keep your license in this sleeve to take advantage of your full driving privileges. For more information, reference SCDMV's brochure *Ready for the Road?* (DMVB-35) which is available on the department's website at www.scdmvonline.com.

Required Non-Commercial License Tests

Where to Take Tests

You must take a vision, knowledge, and skills test when you apply for an original driver's license or upgrade to a different class. You may take vision and knowledge tests at any SCDMV branch. Manuals or other testing aids cannot be used while you take the knowledge test. You will fail the test if you do **any** of the following:

- **Leave** the test room/area before the test is completed
- **Talk** to anyone

- **Take** anything into the test area that may assist you with answers to the questions on the test. Written material or electronic devices of any kind are not allowed in the knowledge test area. Examples of electronic devices are a cell phone, laptop, and tablet reader (such as an iPad or Kindle).

There are also One Stop Driver Training and Testing Programs (also known as third-party testers) available if you are applying for a first-time regular (class D) beginner's permit, driver's license, or motorcycle (class M) license. The SCDMV partners with people, corporations, or governmental subdivisions to administer the SCDMV driving tests. The driver training schools that participate in this program have SCDMV-authorized testers who can administer the knowledge and/or skills tests instead of you having to take the tests at an SCDMV branch office. You can find a list of these **third-party testers** that participate in the One Stop Driver Training Programs on SCDMV's website at www.scdmvonline.com.

NOTICE: *Be prepared because you could be randomly selected by the SCDMV to pass the skills test again before you are issued a driver's license (SC Code Section 56-1-15).*

The first test for every type of license includes a vision, knowledge, and skills test, except for a moped license. The SCDMV does not require a skills test for a moped license.

Taking the Skills Test

Careful study of the South Carolina Driver's Manual will increase your driving confidence and broaden your knowledge of traffic rules and regulations. Your examiner realizes that a driving test will probably be an unusual experience for you and that you might become nervous or uneasy. If you do become apprehensive, please know that your examiner has accompanied many other people who have felt as you may feel and that he or she is riding with you only to make sure that you can control your vehicle and observe the rules of the road. **Your examiner will not try to trick you in any way.** Thousands of people pass this test annually and become licensed SC drivers. If they can do it, so can you. Just relax and do the best you can.

You may hear a skills test called a "skills test" or a "driving test". You need to take a skills test if you do not hold a valid driver's license. You must provide a vehicle for the test. The vehicle must be safe and have all of the following in working condition:

- Headlights & Brakes
- Windshield wipers
- Safety belts
- Turn signals
- Mirrors
- Speedometer
- Defroster
- Horn

The vehicle must have a valid license plate, registration card, and insurance card. The skills test must be postponed if the vehicle is not safe. **You will automatically fail if you do not use your seat belt.**

You should bring **all** of the following items to your test:

- Old license or beginner's permit (if you have one)
- A licensed driver
- Vehicle liability insurance information from a company licensed to do business in SC

An SCDMV employee will test you. You and the employee are the only people allowed in or around the vehicle. Your test includes all of the following:

- Vision test; *If you wear corrective lenses (glasses or contact lenses), bring them or wear them.*
- Knowledge test of traffic laws, road signs, and driving safety rules
- Driving test, if required

During the skills test, you will be required to:

- Turn on your headlights and windshield wipers
- Turn on your turn signals (including four-way flashers)
- Test your brake lights
- Make lane changes
- Make right and left turns
- Identify road signs
- Parallel park
- 100 feet backing
- Park on a hill
- Three point turnabout
- Straight line backing

Failing the Skills Test

If you do not have driving experience and you fail the skills test on your first or second attempt, you must wait two weeks before you can be re-tested, regardless of age.

If you previously held a driver's license and failed the test on your first or second attempt, you must wait one week before you can be re-tested, regardless of age. *A beginner's permit is not considered driving experience.*

If you fail the skills test on your third attempt or more, you must wait 60 days before you can be re-tested, regardless of whether or not you have previous driving experience.

Out-of-State License or Driving on an Existing License

Moving to South Carolina

If you have a valid driver's license or identification (ID) card from another state and permanently move to SC, you must apply for an SC license or ID within ninety days of moving to SC. You must turn in your out-of-state license or ID in order to receive a new one in SC. If your out-of-state license is expired by nine months or more, you must pass the knowledge, skills, and vision tests before you can get an SC license.

You must register your vehicles in SC within forty-five days of moving to SC.

Temporary Resident

If you are moving to SC temporarily, whether a military member, student, or other, you are **not** required to get an SC driver's license for yourself or your dependents. However, you **must** have a valid out-of-state license to drive in SC.

Moving from South Carolina

If you move out of SC, you must turn in your SC driver's license or ID card to your new state of residency when issued a new license or ID. Your new state will notify the SCDMV, and your SC license or ID will be cancelled.

If you are registering a vehicle in a state other than SC, you must transfer your vehicle's liability insurance to that state as well. Before you cancel your SC insurance, turn in your SC license plate to the SCDMV. If you do not return your plate before you cancel your SC insurance, you could owe up to $400 in fees.

Visiting South Carolina

If you are a permanent resident of another state, you can use your valid out-of-state driver's license to drive in SC.

For example, if you are visiting this state from New York, you may drive in this state with your valid out-of-state New York license.

International Visitors

If you are visiting from a non-English speaking country, you are strongly advised to get an International Driving Permit from your home country. An International Driving Permit serves as a language translation to be used with your valid driver's license. It is **not** an actual license but it translates your foreign language license into English. It allows law enforcement officers to read your license.

SC waives the requirement for knowledge and skills testing for an individual who is applying for a first-time SC driver's license and has an out-of-country driving credential (that has not expired) from a country that has a formal reciprocity agreement with SC.

Driver's License Renewal

Renew my Driver's License Online

If you are a US citizen, you may choose to renew your driver's license online for an eight-year license. If you are not a US citizen, you **cannot** renew your driver's license online.

You must meet **all** of the following requirements.

- You have a regular (Class D, E, F, G, M, or any combination of these) license.
- You do **not** have a commercial driver's license.
- Your license is **not** expired.

- Your social security number and the name associated with it matches what is on file with the Social Security Administration.
- You have **not** received more than five points on your record in the last two years.
- Your license is **not** suspended or subject to be suspended.
- You did **not** renew your license by mail or online during the last renewal period.
- You are **not** a Convicted Violent Offender in the SCDMV system.
- You do **not** currently have a conditional or special restricted license.

To renew your Driver's License online at www.scdmvonline.com, you must provide identifying information to log in. At the end of the process, you must pay for your new license with a valid credit card.

The SCDMV will use your current photograph and signature and will mail your new license to the address on file. It will take seven to ten business days to receive your renewed license in the mail.

Renew my Driver's License by Mail

If you are a US citizen, you may choose to renew your driver's license through the mail for an eight-year license. If you are not a US citizen, you **cannot** renew your driver's license by mail.

You must meet **all** of the same requirements listed above for online renewals and you must complete the Driver's License Renewal Application (SCDMV Form DL-63) application. Mail your completed application and a check or money order for $25 (do not mail cash) made out to the SCDMV, to:

SCDMV Alternative Media
PO Box 1498
Blythewood, SC 29016-0035

Mail your application and payment at least three weeks before your expiration date. If you renew by mail, the SCDMV will use the same photograph and signature on your current license.

Renew my Driver's License in Person

You must do **all** of the following to renew at a branch:

- Provide the company name of your vehicle insurance
- Pay $25 for the license

You must pass a knowledge test if you have received more than five points against your driving record in the last two years.

Renewing an Expired Driver's License

Do **not** drive with an expired driver's license. If your license has been expired for **less than** nine months, you may renew it at an SCDMV branch without testing.

If your driver's license is expired by nine months or more, you **must** visit an SCDMV branch, pass a knowledge test and a skills test, provide current proof of address, and any proof of identity documents that may not be on file.

Loss of Driving Privileges

How the Point System Works

You may earn points against your SC driver's license when you violate traffic violations, which include violations committed outside of the state.

Certain traffic violations are assigned points. If you are convicted of a traffic violation in SC or in any other state, that information will be sent to the SCDMV and be posted to your record.

You may receive points on your driving record if you do **any** of the following:

- Break the law in this state or any state
- Receive a military court-martial traffic convictions

Your record contains all the convictions you have received from traffic violations and the number of points charged against you under the point system. Points are reduced by half after one year from the violation date on the ticket. For example, if you received four points on your record in June, the points would be reduced to two points in June of the next year.

If you are 15 or 16, the SCDMV will send you a letter to drive more carefully when you receive two points and/or four points on your driving record. If you continue to break the law **or** if you already have additional convictions, the department has not yet received, you could lose your driving privileges.

If you are 17 or older and have six or more points on your driving record, the SCDMV will send you a letter to drive more carefully. If your point total reaches 12 or more, your license will be suspended.

Driver's License Suspension for Excessive Points

If you hold a beginner's permit, conditional or special restricted driver's license and you accumulate six or more points, your driving privileges will be suspended for having excessive points. If you are suspended for having excessive points, completing the National Safety Defensive Drive Course, or its equivalent, will **not** reinstate the suspension.

The points that resulted in an excessive point's suspension can also be used in a point system suspension.

Certain violations, such as driving under the influence, require mandatory license suspensions and are not under the point system.

Defensive Driving Course

If you have points, you may have them reduced if you complete the National Safety Council's Defensive Driving Course or an equivalent. Some defensive driving courses are offered at SCDMV-certified driving schools. To find schools that offer this course, search for ones that are certified for four-point reduction.

- The course **cannot** be completed online.
- The course must be taken in SC.
- The course must be eight hours of classroom training.
- The course must be taken after the date of violation(s).
- A reduction in points may only be made one time in a three-year period.
- If you take a defensive driving course because your license is in danger of being suspended, you must complete the course before the suspension begins. Once the suspension begins, the point reduction will not cancel or reduce the suspension.

License Reinstatement

There are many different types of suspensions. If you have specific questions, call SCDMV's Contact Center 803-896-5000 or visit an SCDMV branch.

Reinstatement Fees

If you have a SC driver's license and owe reinstatement fees, you may pay them online. A $100 reinstatement fee is required for each suspension unless noted otherwise.

Payment Plan

If you owe more than $300 in reinstatement fees, you may be eligible for the payment plan. You must qualify for participation and follow all payment plan rules.

Provisional Driver's License

If your driving privileges are suspended for first offense Driving Under the Influence (DUI) or Driving with an Unlawful Alcohol Concentration (DUAC), you may be eligible for a six-month provisional driver's license as long as you meet **all** of the following requirements, based on when the violation happened.

- You must have or have had a valid SC driver's license or be exempt.
- You must have met all requirements for prior suspensions, revocations, and cancellations.
- If the DUI or DUAC violation was **on October 1, 2014 or later**, you must have had a BAC of 0.14 percent or less.
- You must have **no other suspensions** after the DUI or DUAC suspension **except** for the following, as long as they are from the same DUI or DUAC violation: implied consent, implied consent under 21, BAC of 0.02 percent or greater, BAC of 0.15 percent or greater, or alcohol violation.
- You must be enrolled in the Alcohol and Drug Safety Action Program (ADSAP).
- You must pay $100 for a provisional license.

Route Restricted Driver's License

If you are not a US citizen, you are **not** eligible for this license unless you have permanent resident alien status.

If you receive a route-restricted license, you may drive a non-commercial vehicle while driving:

- To and from your place of employment, education, or residence
- To and from an Alcohol and Drug Safety Action Program (ADSAP)
- To and from a court-ordered drug program

You must keep a copy of the approved route with you.

Your route-restricted license is valid for the length of the suspension.

You may **only** receive **one** route-restricted license in your lifetime for the following suspensions:

- Accident Judgment
- Alcohol Violation
- Blood Alcohol Concentration (BAC) of .15
- Controlled Substance
- Failure to Stop for a Blue Light
- False Insurance Certification
- Implied Consent
- Misrepresentation of Identity

If you have been suspended for not paying child support or driving under suspension (1st or 2nd offense within five years), you **may** be eligible for more than one route restricted license in your lifetime. If approved, a route restricted license costs $100.

To apply for a route-restricted license, complete the Application for a Route Restricted Driver's License Application (SCDMV form DL-127) and mail it to this address below:

SCDMV Driver Records
PO Box 1498
Blythewood, SC 29016-0028

Temporary Alcohol License

You may be eligible for a Temporary Alcohol license (TAL) if you have **one** of the following suspensions **and** have filed for an administrative hearing within 30 days:

- Implied Consent
- Implied Consent under 21
- Blood Alcohol Concentration (BAC) of 0.15 percent
- BAC of 0.02 percent or more under 21

While the results of your hearing are pending, you may receive a TAL for $100. You will be able to use your TAL until the SCDMV receives the results of the hearing.

If your suspension is sustained or continues to be in place, you should return the TAL to an SCDMV branch. You may be eligible for a route restricted driver's license.

If your suspension is rescinded or overturned, you **must** return the TAL before you are able to apply for your regular license.

Section 2

State Laws and Rules of the Road

This Section Covers
• State Laws
• State Rules of the Road

State Laws

This section highlights a few state laws of interest to drivers. It does not address every law.

Selective Service

You must complete the Supplement for SC Credential Selective Service Requirements (SCDMV form 447-SEL) if you are a male US citizen or an immigrant who is less than twenty-six years of age when applying for a beginner's permit, driver's license or identification card. The SCDMV is required to send your name, address, date of birth, gender, Social Security number, and date of application to the US Selective Service when you reach the age of 18 unless you physically surrender your beginner's permit, driver's license, or identification card before your 18th birthday.

SC Code Section 56-1-125

Organ Donation

You may register to be an organ/tissue donor when you apply for or renew your SC driver's license, beginner's permit, or identification card. If you choose to register, your identity information will be added to the SC Donor Registry and a red heart will be added to your license, beginner's permit, or ID. When you choose to be an organ or tissue donor, you are entering into a legally binding agreement as outlined under the SC Uniform Anatomical Gift Act.

If you choose to be an organ donor before your 18th birthday, your parent or legal guardian shall make the final decision regarding donation. If you change your decision about being an organ donor in the future or wish to update your information on the registry, visit the website for Donate Life SC at www.donatelifesc.org.

SC Code Section 44-43-320

Littering is Against the Law

It is against the law to throw trash along the streets and highways. Offenders can be arrested and fined. You can be fined for litter law violations and also be directed to pick up litter along the roadsides under supervision of the court.

Please take pride in SC and its beauty by not littering the highways.

An idea is to keep a litter container in your vehicle at all times. Paper cups, candy wrappers, bottles, and other litter can be placed in this container. Then, when the container is filled, you may dispose of it in a trash can or another appropriate litter receptacle. **Cigarettes and cigarette butts are considered litter and should be kept inside your vehicle until they can be disposed of properly.**

SC Code Section 16-11-700

State Rules of the Road

This section highlights a few, but not all, rules of the road.

Golf Carts

You must be at least 16 years old and have a valid driver's license to drive a golf cart. A golf cart must have an SCDMV-issued permit/registration decal affixed to it. You may operate a golf cart during the day as follows:

- within four miles of the address on the registration certificate

Handwritten margin notes: "o NOT t any longer your r throw ything It the window ash, inks, e, ti when ou are riving."

Handwritten margin note (right): "if you have to empty a drink, wait to do it when you stop."

- within four miles of the gate of a gated community
- only on secondary streets and highways with posted speed limits of thirty-five miles an hour or less.

SC Code Section 56-2-105

Commercial Motor Vehicles

Reference SCDMV's *Commercial Driver's License Manual* for information on this topic.

Large Non-Commercial Vehicles

Reference SCDMV's *Large Non-Commercial & Recreational Vehicles Driver's Manual.*

Mopeds

Reference SCDMV's *Motorcycle & Moped Operator's Manual* for information on this topic.

Motorcycles

Reference SCDMV's *Motorcycle & Moped Operator's Manual* for information on this topic.

Recreational Vehicles

Reference SCDMV's *Large Non-Commercial & Recreational Vehicles Driver's Manual.*

Section 3

Be in Shape to Drive

This Section Covers
• Vision
• Fatigue
• Driver Distractions
• Aggressive Driving
• Alcohol, Other Drugs, and Driving
• Emotions
• Driving Tips for Older Drivers

Driving is one of the most risky activities you may choose to do during your lifetime. Your ability to drive safely depends on good health and making correct decisions.

Vision

Good vision is important for safe driving. If you cannot see clearly, you will have difficulty identifying traffic and roadway conditions, spotting potential trouble, and responding to problems in a timely manner.

Because seeing well is so important to safe driving, it is best if you have your eyes checked regularly by a licensed eye care professional. If you are required to wear corrective lenses:

- Always wear them when driving.
- Avoid using dark or tinted corrective lenses at night, even if you think they help with glare. These types of lenses reduce the light you need to see clearly.
- If you use bioptic telescopic lenses to operate a motor vehicle, you must submit vision screening documentation (Low Vision Acuity Screening for Non-Commercial Beginner Permits or Driver's Licenses (SCDMV form 412-LV) to SCDMV's Driver Improvement unit every year.

You may be required to pass an eye test in a branch office with a mechanical device (orthorater) that is designed to test your ability to read from a distance or you can have a licensed eye care professional test your vision. A licensed eye care professional must test your vision if you fail SCDMV's test or choose not to be tested in the branch office. Licensed eye care professionals must complete the appropriate SCDMV vision screening form. The Report of Vision Screening for Non-Commercial Beginner Permit or Driver's License (SCDMV form 412-NC) is to be completed by an eye care professional for non-commercial drivers. A vision screening is required for non-commercial drivers under these conditions:

- The first time you apply for an SC beginner's permit or driver's license.
- If you want to have a corrective lens restriction code "A" removed from your license.
- When renewing your driver's license or beginner's permit beginning October 1, 2020.
- If you are surrendering an out-of-state license to get a SC license.

The minimum vision standards do not require a greater degree of vision than 20/40 corrected in one eye. A restriction will be added to your beginner's permit or driver's license if your vision is corrected to meet the minimum standards with the use of corrective lenses (glasses or contact lenses). It is unlawful for you to drive a motor vehicle without the use of corrective lenses if they are required to meet the minimum standards.

If your vision improves to the extent that corrective lenses are no longer necessary you must provide a certificate of vision examination from a licensed eye care professional showing the new vision readings.

You must then have your license renewed to have the restriction removed.

Fatigue

Fatigue is physical or mental tiredness that can be caused by physical or mental strain, repetitive tasks, illness, or lack of sleep. Fatigue can affect your vision and increase the time to make decisions. Avoid driving if you are tired or fatigued. You do not want to fall asleep when you are driving.

Here are some tips for before you take a trip:

- Get adequate sleep—most people need 7 to 9 hours per day to maintain proper alertness throughout their awake hours.
- Plan to stop about every 100 miles or 2 hours during long trips.
- Arrange for a travel companion—someone to watch your driving.
- Check the labels of your medications and be aware if they cause drowsiness.
- Do not use alcohol and other drugs before or when driving.

Ways to Avoid Fatigue

- If you start feeling tired stop driving and pull off at the next exit or rest area to take a 15 to 20 minute nap or find a place to sleep for the night.
- Try not to drive late at night.
- The best way to avoid fatigue is to get plenty of rest.

Driver Distractions

A distraction is anything that takes your attention away from driving. Distracted driving can cause collisions, resulting in injury, death, or property damage. Taking your eyes off the road or hands off the steering wheel presents obvious driving risks. **Mental activities that take your mind away from driving are just as dangerous.**

When driving:

- Do not use cell phones. It is unlawful in SC to use a wireless electronic communication device while operating a motor vehicle if it requires the use of either hand.
  SC Code Section 56-5-3890
- Avoid arguments and stressful or emotional conversations with passengers.
- Avoid eating while driving.
- Be sure children are properly and safely buckled up.
- Properly secure pets in a pet carrier or portable kennel.

You must pay attention to the task of driving. You are responsible for operating your vehicle in a safe manner.

Aggressive Driving   *AKA ROAD RAGE*

Aggressive driving occurs when an individual intentionally commits an action that endangers other persons or property.

Some behaviors typically associated with aggressive driving include speeding, following too closely, unsafe lane changes, improperly (or not) signaling, and failing *tailgating, break-checking*

Also Honking horn aggressively or flipping the bird

If someone is being aggressive with you, LET THEM PASS you. It's not worth your life.

Do NOT flip someone off PPlc are CRAZY

to obey traffic control devices (stop signs, yield signs, traffic signals, railroad grade cross signals, etc.).

Concentrate on your driving. Be patient and courteous to other road users. *Being a jerk v not worth your life*

Alcohol, Other Drugs, and Driving

If you suspect you're behind a drunk driver, Can 911 (w/siri) GIVE THEM PLENTY OF ROOM

Alcohol and other impairing drugs are involved in approximately 40% of all traffic collisions in which someone is killed each year. If you drink alcohol or use other impairing drugs and drive, even a little, your chances of being in a collision are much greater than if you did not drink any alcohol or use any other drugs.

If You are Under 21

If you are under the age of 21, it is illegal to purchase, possess, or drink alcoholic beverages. Alcohol and other impairing drugs affect a person's ability to perceive his or her surroundings, react to emergencies, and skillfully operate a motor vehicle. For new drivers learning complex skills, the effects of alcohol and other impairing drugs is greater. All states have "zero tolerance" laws (no alcohol in the circulatory system) or similar laws for drivers under the age of 21.

Effects of Alcohol and Other Impairing Drugs

Alcohol and other impairing drugs reduces your:

- **Judgment**: Judgment is a brain-centered activity that stores all of your experiences and knowledge so it can be used quickly when you face a new problem.

- **Vision**: The most important sense you use in driving is vision. Alcohol blurs your vision, slows your ability to focus, causes double vision, and reduces the ability to judge distance, speed, and the movement of other vehicles. Vision is impacted at 0.02 percent blood alcohol content (BAC) for all drivers.

- **Color distinction**: Alcohol reduces your ability to distinguish colors.
- **Reaction time**: Alcohol slows your ability to process information and respond to the task of driving.

The best advice is not to drive a vehicle of any kind if you have consumed alcohol or other drugs. Impairment starts with the first drink. Even one drink of alcohol can affect a person's ability to operate a motor vehicle. With one or more drinks in the bloodstream, a person is visibly impaired and could be arrested for driving under the influence of alcohol or other drugs. Never let a friend or relative drive if he or she has been drinking.

Alcohol and the Law

BAC is the percentage of alcohol in relation to the amount of blood in your body. If you have a blood alcohol concentration (BAC) of 0.05 percent or higher, you are in violation of the law and must not operate a motor vehicle. If you are arrested for drinking and driving, the penalties are severe. If you have a BAC of 0.08 percent or more, your driver's license and driving privileges may be suspended. Even under 0.08 percent, you are still impaired. Under the law, you can still be convicted for driving impaired.

If you are under 21 years of age and register a BAC of 0.02 percent or greater, your privilege to drive will be suspended immediately for three months. If you have prior violations of DUI, Felony DUI, Implied Consent or a BAC of 0.02 percent or greater in the last five years of the first offense, your driving privilege will immediately be suspended for six months. If you refuse to take the test for intoxicants and it is your first offense, you will immediately lose your driving privileges for six months. If you have prior violations of DUI, Felony DUI, Implied Consent or a BAC of 0.02 percent or greater in the last five years of the first offense, your driving privilege will immediately be suspended for one year.

An alcohol concentration test measures how much alcohol is in your system and is usually determined by a breath, blood, or urine test. You are required to take a BAC test if asked by a police officer due to SC's implied consent law. SC's implied consent law is based on the principle that when you get your driver's license, you  have implicitly consented to a lawfully- requested test to determine the alcohol content of your blood, breath, or urine if suspected of impaired driving. You can lose your driver's license or driving privileges if you refuse to take a BAC test.

Although implied consent laws vary by state, the law applies to the state where you were arrested, not the state where you got your license.

If you are convicted of driving under the influence in SC and it is your first conviction, you may be fined from $400 to $1000 plus court costs. You could be sentenced to forty-eight hours to thirty days in jail, and your license could be suspended for 6 months. Legal fees and insurance increases can exceed $10,000. For second and subsequent convictions, the penalties are much worse.

Other Impairing Drugs and Driving

Besides alcohol, many other drugs can affect your ability to drive safely. These drugs can have effects similar to, or worse than, those of alcohol. This is true of many prescription drugs and many of the drugs you can buy over the counter without a prescription.

Over-the-Counter Drugs

Over-the-counter drugs taken for headaches, colds, allergies, or those to calm nerves can make you drowsy and affect your driving. Pep pills, "uppers", and diet pills can make you feel nervous, dizzy, unable to concentrate, and may affect your vision. Check the label on the product before you take an over-the-counter drug for warnings about its effect. If you are not sure if it is safe to take the drug and drive, ask your doctor or pharmacist about any known side effects.

Prescription Drugs

Some prescription drugs can impact your driving and can affect your reflexes, judgment, vision, and alertness in ways similar to alcohol. Many prescription drugs have an impact on driving safely. Check the label on the prescription and packaging before you take a drug for warnings about its effect. If you are not sure if it is safe to take the drug and drive, ask your doctor or pharmacist about any known side effects.

Illegal Drugs

Illegal drugs can impact your driving and may affect your reflexes, judgment, vision, and alertness in ways similar to alcohol. If you are convicted in SC of a drug violation while driving and it is your first conviction, you may be fined from $400 to $1000 plus court costs. You could be sentenced from forty-eight hours to thirty days in jail, and your license could be suspended for 6 months. You may also be subject to other criminal penalties. For second and subsequent convictions, the penalties are much worse.

Combining Alcohol and Other Impairing Drugs

Never drink alcohol while you are taking other drugs. These drugs could multiply the effects of alcohol or have additional effects of their own. No one is able to drink alcohol or use other impairing drugs and still operate a vehicle safely.

Emotions *This is Huge.*

Emotions can increase your risk of driving safely by interfering with your ability to think, creating a lack of attention, and interrupting your ability to process information. You may not be able to drive well when you are experiencing extreme levels of any emotion.

There are ways of dealing with your emotions:

- If you are angry or worried, it is best to give yourself time to "cool off". A short walk or nap may help. It is best to stay off the road until your symptoms have passed.

- Give yourself extra time for your driving trip. Leave several minutes early.

- Have someone else drive.

Driving Tips for Older Drivers

The aging process can affect our driving ability. These are some problems that may face an older driver in traffic:

- As age progresses, hearing and eyesight are often less keen.

Are you trying to die?!

Always be kind to those on the road. You never know what they are going through.

- Judgment may be slower. It may take longer to recognize traffic situations and to make the necessary decisions.

- Physical dexterity may be weakened. Older people may not have the same ability to act with speed in an emergency as they used to have.

- The older driver may not realize that new rules and regulations are being continually introduced.

Here's a chance to check your own driving. These are common causes of trouble among older drivers. If two or three of the points apply to you, it may be time to modify your driving habits or give up driving entirely. Don't risk hurting yourself or others. Talk with a doctor about any concerns you have about your health and driving. Your doctor may determine that your driving skills be assessed by a SCDMV examiner.

- You need two or three tries when parking your vehicle parallel to the curb in a parking space.

- You encountered difficulty distinguishing between objects, such as a hydrant and a small child, when driving at night.

- The glare from headlights of approaching vehicles cause prolonged discomfort to your eyes at night.

- You have trouble maintaining the pace of other vehicles or they seem to be passing you all the time.

- It takes you quite a long time to get going again after the light has turned green.

- You are getting an increasing number of minor scrapes (such as from your garage door) or dents on your vehicle.

- You miss STOP signs, highway signs, and other traffic indicators.

- You find yourself becoming confused when unexpected or unfamiliar things happen while you are driving.

- You have trouble making out objects that are a few feet away.

- When a vehicle is approaching you on the road, you have trouble judging how far away it is at a given moment.

- When you are looking straight ahead in the driver's seat, you have difficulty seeing the sides of the road.

Section 4

Before You Drive

Inspecting Your Vehicle

When it comes to road safety, you can't control other drivers or road conditions, but you can control the proper maintenance of your vehicle and tires.

Collisions due to tire maintenance are preventable and simple steps can save lives. Driving on under-inflated or over-inflated tires or on tires with low tread can lead to safety issues on the road.

Check Tire Pressure with a Pressure Gauge Monthly

- Buy a tire pressure gauge if you don't have one already.

- Open your vehicle door. On the inside doorframe, you should see a sticker. Make a note of what the PSI number is on the sticker. PSI means Pounds per Square Inch which is the measurement for tire pressure.

- Remove the cap from the valve stem and press the air pressure gauge evenly onto the valve stem to get an accurate reading (make sure you check when they are cold).

- Compare the number on the gauge with the number you wrote down. If the number on your gauge is higher than the number on the doorframe, let air out of your tires. If the number on your gauge is lower than the number on the doorframe, inflate your tires until the numbers match.

Check Tread Depth with a Penny

- Hold a penny with Lincoln's body between your thumb and forefinger.

- Place the penny with Lincoln's head going first into the deepest-looking groove.

- Can you see all of his head? If yes, your tires are too worn—don't drive on them. Make sure to get them replaced.

bald tires, or tires with no or low tread are extremely dangerous b/c they cannot grip the road properly.

YOU NEED NEW TIRES

YOUR TIRES ARE GOOD

Take the Penny Test

LIBERTY

2010

Adjusting Seat and Mirrors

You should sit upright with your back against the seat and feet on the floor. Improper seating positions, such as slouching, can result in reduced effectiveness of the vehicle's restraint 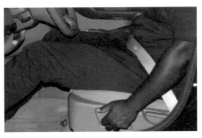 system. Adjust your seat and mirrors before you start to drive. This enables you to see clearly and have full control of the vehicle's foot pedals and steering wheel. This also allows appropriate space for airbag deployment.

- Your foot should be able to pivot smoothly from brake to accelerator while your heel stays on the floor.
- The top of the steering wheel should be no higher than the top of your shoulders.
- There should be at least 10 inches between your chest and the steering wheel. Do not move the seat so far forward that you cannot easily steer and do not recline the seat.
- Head restraints are designed to prevent whiplash. Adjust head restraints so the head restraint contacts the **back** of your head and **not below the level of your ears**.

Adjusting Your Mirrors

The rearview mirror (the interior mirror on the windshield) is the primary mirror to view the rear. Adjust your rearview mirror so that it frames the rear window. You should be able to see traffic flow to the rear of the vehicle with the rearview mirror. If you have a day/night mirror, make sure it is set for the time of day you are driving.

Adjust outside mirrors to reduce blind spots (areas where your view is obstructed) and to provide maximum visibility to the sides and rear of the vehicle. To reduce blind spots, you are encouraged to use the following method for adjusting your outside mirrors.

Enhanced Mirror Settings

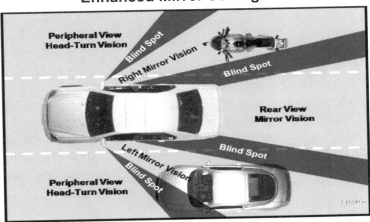

- To set the left side mirror, the driver must rest his or her head against the closed window on the left and adjust the mirror so the rear edge of the vehicle barely shows.

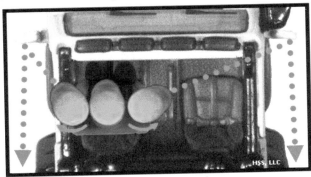

- To set the right side mirror, the driver should lean to the right so his or her head is directly below the rearview mirror or above the center console. The mirror should be adjusted so that the edge of the right side of your vehicle can barely be seen.
- The driver will not see the left and right sides of the vehicle when glancing in the outside mirrors; however, this adjustment adds 12 to 16 degrees of additional viewing area to each side of the vehicle.

Using Safety Belts

Always fasten your safety belt and make sure all your passengers are using safety belts or child restraints. Studies have shown that if you are in a collision while using safety belts, your chances of injury or death are greatly reduced. Safety belts keep you from being thrown from the vehicle and helps the driver keep control of the vehicle.

South Carolina has a primary safety belt enforcement law. Under the primary law, a law enforcement officer has the authority to stop a driver if the officer has a clear and unobstructed  view of a driver or occupant of a motor vehicle not wearing a safety belt or not secured in a child restraint system.

It is important to wear the safety belt correctly.

- A shoulder harness is worn across the shoulder and chest with minimal, if any, slack. Do **not** wear the shoulder harness under the arm or behind the back.  Wearing the harness the wrong way could result in serious internal injuries in a collision.

- Adjust the lap belt so it is snug and lies low across your hips after fastening. Otherwise, in a collision, you could slide out of the belt, resulting in possible injury or death.

Safety belts should be worn even if the vehicle is equipped with air bags.

Air Bags

Air bags are supplemental restraints and are designed to work best in combination with safety belts. In a collision, air bags and safety belts reduce the chance that your head and upper body will strike some part of the vehicle's interior. Safety belts help to properly position your body to maximize the air bag's benefits and help restrain you during collisions. It is extremely important that safety belts are always worn, even in air bag-equipped vehicles.

Read your vehicle owner's manual for specific information about the air bags in your vehicle.

Child Passenger Safety Laws

If using a child safety seat, you must install it properly in your vehicle and use it correctly. You must never place a rear-facing child safety seat in front of an air bag.

- Children age seven and younger must sit in a car seat in the back seat of the vehicle to avoid injury from an air bag in the event of a collision.

- Read your vehicle owner's manual and child restraint directions for more specific information on the child restraint system in your vehicle.

- If you would like to view the law regarding child passenger safety you may visit the Buckle Up, South Carolina website at: https://scdps.sc.gov/buckleupsc

  SC Code Section 56-5-6410

Rear-Facing Car Seat	Forward-Facing Car Seat	Booster Seat	Seat Belt
An infant under two must be secured in a rear-facing car seat in a rear seat of the vehicle until the child exceeds the height or weight limit allowed by the manufacturer of the car seat.	A child at least age two **or** under who has outgrown the manufacturer's height or weight limits for a rear-facing car seat must be secured in a forward-facing car seat in a rear seat of the vehicle until the child exceeds the height or weight requirements of the forward-facing car seat.	Children at least age four who have outgrown their forward-facing car seat must be secured by a booster seat in a rear seat of the vehicle until the child can meet the height and fit requirements for an adult safety seat belt. Lap **and** shoulder belts must be used to secure this car seat.	A child at least age 8 **or** at least 57 inches tall may be restrained by an adult safety belt *if the child can be secured properly by an adult safety seat belt.*

Secure Your Load

Driving with an unsecured load (property being transported) is both against the law and extremely dangerous. A driver who fails to properly secure their load is guilty of a misdemeanor and may face a fine and the cost to have the substance of their load cleaned up. A load must be securely fastened and is only considered secure when nothing can slide, shift, fall, or sift onto the roadway or become airborne.

To secure a load in or on your vehicle or trailer:
- Tie it down with rope, netting, or straps directly to your vehicle or trailer.
- Consider covering the entire load with a sturdy tarp or netting.
- Do not overload your vehicle or trailer.
- Always double check your load to make sure it is secure.
- Remember that animals should also be properly secured.

Before you drive, ask yourself these questions:
- Is there any chance of debris or cargo falling or blowing out or off of my vehicle?
- Is the load secured at the back, sides, and top?
- What would happen to the load if I had to brake suddenly, hit a bump, or another vehicle hit me?
- Would I feel safe if I were driving behind my vehicle?

While you won't be driving w/ an unsecured load, the driver in front (beside) of you might. *KNOW* what to look for and be aware.

Section 5
Basic Driving

This Section Covers
- Starting the Engine
- Moving the Vehicle
- Stopping the Vehicle
- Steering
- Backing Up

Starting the Engine

Check the vehicle owner's manual for how to start a vehicle. To start the engine, place your right foot on the brake pedal and check the gear selector lever for park. Place the key  in the ignition and turn the ignition switch to the on position. If the vehicle has an engine start button push and release it. Once the engine is started, check the gauges and if there are any indicator lights on the dashboard that need attention (fuel level, oil level, ABS, air bags, etc.).

Moving the Vehicle

Move the gear selector lever to "D" (drive). Look in front of the vehicle to ensure the path moving forward is safe and check for any traffic or obstacles on the sides, behind, or in any blind spots (by looking over your shoulder). Signal and if safe; move your foot to the accelerator and press gently. Accelerate gradually and smoothly with the top of your foot on the pedal and the heel of your foot on the floor.

Stopping the Vehicle

Check your mirrors for traffic at the rear of your vehicle. Move your foot from the accelerator to the brake pedal.

Press with steady pressure until your vehicle comes to a stop.

Steering

A steering wheel is turned in the direction you want the vehicle to move, whether moving forward or in reverse. Place both hands on the outside of the steering wheel on opposite sides. Your grip on the steering wheel should be firm but gentle. Use your fingers to grip the steering wheel instead of the palms of your hands and keep your thumbs up along the face of the steering wheel. Never turn the wheel while gripping it from the inside of the rim. You cannot control the car this way.

The proper grip on the steering wheel of a vehicle is extremely important. Think of the steering wheel as the face of a clock. Place your left hand at the 7 to 9 o'clock position and your right hand at the 3 to 5 o'clock position. Your grip should be firm but not too tight. Both of your hands should remain on the steering wheel at all times except when one hand is performing some other necessary function of driving such as shifting gears, turning on the windshield wipers, or giving hand signals for turning, slowing or stopping.

It takes practice to get a "feel" of the vehicle you are handling. When you are first learning to handle your car or truck choose lightly traveled rural roads, when possible. After you feel you can steer the vehicle accurately, making the tiny adjustments that are constantly necessary in steering, then you will be ready to practice other driving techniques such as turning and parking.

Hand-to-Hand Steering

Use hand-to-hand steering, commonly called push/pull steering, when turning the wheel during normal driving activity going forward above 10-15 mph. When using hand-to-hand steering your left hand grasps the wheel between 7 and 8 o'clock and your right hand grasps the wheel between 4 and 5 o'clock. Depending on the direction of the turn, your right or left hand pushes the wheel up and the opposite hand slides up, grasps the wheel and pulls down to continue the turn. While the pulling hand moves down, the hand that initially pushed up slides back toward its original position to make adjustments as needed.

The driver should use the area on the wheel between 11 and 8 o'clock with the left hand and the area on the wheel between 1 and 8 o'clock with the right hand regardless of the direction of the turn. Simply reverse the hand-to-hand process to bring the vehicle into your intended path.

With your left hand positioned in the area between 7 and 9 o'clock and your right hand positioned in the area between 3 and 5 o'clock there tends to be less muscle stress; therefore, less steering to cause any weaving in a lane. With your arms next to your body, it is more natural to keep both of your hands on the wheel at all times. Since your hands and arms never cross over the steering wheel, there is less chance of injury to your face, hands, and arms in the event of a frontal crash when a vehicle is equipped with a driver's side air bag. This is the preferred method of

Basic Driving

steering, 2 and 10 o'clock is not recommended because it can be dangerous in vehicles equipped with airbags.

Hand-Over-Hand Steering

Use hand-over-hand steering when turning the wheel at low speeds, such as at an intersection or when parking the vehicle. When using hand-over-hand steering, your left hand grasps the steering wheel between 8 and 9 o'clock and your right hand grasps the wheel between 3 and 4 o'clock. Depending on the direction of the turn, use the right top third of the steering wheel to move the wheel to the right and use the left top third of the wheel to move the wheel to the left. This process is repeated as necessary. Simply reverse the hand-over-hand process to bring the vehicle into your intended path.

One Hand Steering

Use one hand steering only when backing up or operating vehicle controls (wipers, flashers, lights, etc.) that require a temporary reach from the steering wheel. The placement of one hand on the steering wheel at all times is critical to vehicle balance, steering reversals, and to avoid potential injury. When the driver is required to reach for an operating control, it is important to keep the other hand in the normal vehicle operating position of 8-9 o'clock or 3-4 o'clock, depending on the steering wheel design. This maintains vehicle stability, reduces steering reversals, and allows for additional steering efforts as needed. The only time that 12 o'clock is recommended is when backing a vehicle to the left or right and the driver has to turn in the seat in order to see the path of travel to the rear.

Backing Up

Follow these steps to back a vehicle up safely:

- Check behind the vehicle before you get in it. Children and small objects cannot be seen from the driver's seat.
- Place your foot on the brake and shift to reverse.
- Grasp the steering wheel at the 12 o'clock position with your left hand.
- Place your right arm on the back of the passenger seat to the right and look directly through the rear window.

- Occasionally check your mirrors when backing up but keep in mind that these mirrors do not show the area immediately behind your vehicle. If your vehicle is equipped with a rearview camera, occasionally check it while backing up.
- Accelerate gently and smoothly, keeping your speed slow. Your vehicle is much harder to steer while you are backing up.

- Steer slightly in the direction the rear of the vehicle should move. If backing up while turning, make quick checks to the front and sides.
- Continue looking to the rear until coming to a complete stop.

Section 6

Rules of the Road

This Section Covers

- Yielding Right-of-Way
- Traffic Control Devices
- Traffic Signals
- Traffic Signs
- Pavement Markings
- Other Lane Controls

Yielding Right-of-Way

Yielding right-of-way rules provide drivers with guidance for situations when other drivers or pedestrians are present. These rules determine which driver should yield the right-of-way and the sequence for entering and driving through an intersection or other driving scenarios.

Although yielding right-of-way rules provide a guide to determine who should yield the right-of-way, no one should assume he or she automatically has the right-of-way. The situation and circumstances at each intersection must always be considered.

You should yield the right-of-way to:

- **pedestrians, bicyclists, and other drivers who are still in the intersection;**

First Car Rule

- the driver who is at or arrives before you at the intersection (see First Car Rule image);

- drivers in the opposing traffic lane when you are making a left turn;

- the driver on your right at a four-way intersection controlled by stop signs if both of you arrive at the intersection at the same time (see Same Time Rule image);

Same Time Rule

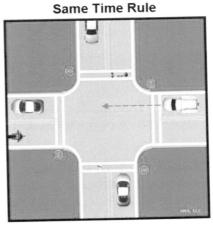

- drivers on a public highway if you are entering the highway from a driveway or a private road; and

- drivers already on a limited access or interstate highway if you are on the entrance or acceleration ramp.

Traffic Control Devices

Traffic control devices include traffic signals, signs, pavement markings, and directions provided by law enforcement, highway personnel, and school crossing guards.

Traffic Signals

Traffic signals are lights that tell you when or where you should stop and go. Traffic lights are usually at intersections and illuminate red, yellow, and green from the top to the bottom, when on the same traffic device. There are some intersections, and other locations, where there are lights of only one color (green, yellow, or red). In some metropolitan areas traffic lights are horizontal instead of vertical, and the red light is on the left, the yellow light is in the middle, and the green light is on the right.

GREEN Traffic Light—This means you may go through the intersection if it is clear to do so, with caution.

YELLOW Traffic Light—A yellow caution light follows the green signal and is a warning that the signal is about to change to the red stop signal. Therefore, you should stop your vehicle and wait for the next green light. If you are already in the intersection, clear the intersection as quickly as possible. You must observe and allow for errors made by other drivers - side, front and rear – when you are approaching a yellow light.

RED Traffic Light—This means stop before entering the intersection. You must wait behind the stop line, crosswalk, or intersection until the traffic light turns green. An exception to this rule permits traffic facing a red signal to turn right except where a sign prohibits a right turn on red. When turning on red you must stop before entering the crosswalk on the near side of the turn and yield right-of-way to pedestrians who are lawfully within and adjacent to the crosswalk and to other traffic lawfully using the intersection.

Flashing YELLOW Traffic Light—This means slow down and proceed with caution. You should be prepared to stop for any traffic flow that may be entering the intersection.

Flashing RED Traffic Light—This means you must stop behind a stop line, crosswalk, or intersection before entering and use the same procedure as you would at a stop sign, by coming to a complete stop. Look both ways before entering the intersection and yield right-of-way, if applicable.

Traffic Signs

Traffic signs tell you about traffic rules, hazards, roadway location, roadway directions, and the location of roadway services. The shape, color, symbols, and words on these signs give clues to the type of information they provide. This section highlights a few signs of interest to drivers. It does not address every sign.

Warning Signs—These signs tell a driver of possible danger that might be ahead, such as warning you to slow down and be prepared to stop or notifying you of a hazard or special situation on the roadway that is ahead. These signs are usually yellow with black lettering or symbols and are diamond shaped. Some warning signs may be fluorescent yellow, such as school zones, school crossings, and pedestrian crossings. Some common warning signs are shown below.

Cross Road Ahead

Side Road Ahead

T-Intersection Ahead

Y-Intersection Ahead

Curvy Road Ahead

Right Curve

Divided Highway Begins	Divided Highway Ends	Lane Ends

Merging Traffic	Added Lane	Traffic Signal Ahead

Stop Sign Ahead	Sharp Curve Ahead	Advisory Speed Around Curve

School Crossing	Pedestrian Crossing	Share the Road with Bicycles

Bicycle Crossing	Slippery When Wet	

Railroad Crossing Warning Signs—Many railroad crossings have signs or signals to caution you about highway-railroad grade crossings. Some common railroad crossing warning signs and signals are shown below.

- A round yellow warning sign with an "X" symbol and black "RR" letters is placed along the road **before** a highway-railroad grade crossing. The sign cautions you to slow down, look, and listen for a train or railroad vehicle, and be prepared to stop if a train is approaching.

- A white, X-shaped sign with "Railroad Crossing" printed on it is located **at** the highway-railroad grade crossing. When a train or railroad vehicle is approaching the intersection, you must stop behind the stop line or before the intersection until the intersection is clear.

- At highway-railroad grade crossings with more than one train track, the number of tracks will be posted. These signs warn you that there is more than one track and there may be more than one train or railroad vehicle crossing. **Not all highway-railroad grade crossings with more than one train track will have these signs, so it is important to check for more than one track, train, or railroad vehicle at each highway-railroad grade crossing.**

Not all railroad grade crossings have lights.

When you need to cross railroad tracks, look both ways and cross the tracks quickly, without stopping. If a train is crossing the highway, you must wait to cross a highway-railroad grade crossing until the train is well down the track or railroad devices (such as lights and gates) indicate it is safe to cross. If you are approaching railroad tracks and you need to stop for traffic or a signal, stop at the stop line before the railroad tracks. If your vehicle ever gets stuck on a track, contact the emergency phone number listed on the blue sign and provide the crossing information.

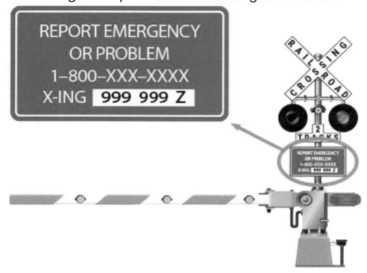

Work Zone Signs—These are generally diamond- or rectangular-shaped and orange with black letters or symbols. These construction, maintenance, or emergency operation signs alert you to work zones ahead and warn you that people are working on or near the roadway. These warnings include workers ahead, a reduced speed zone, detours, slow-moving construction equipment, and poor or suddenly changing road surfaces.

Flagger Ahead	Workers Ahead	Road Construction Ahead

One Lane Road Ahead	Detour

In work zones, traffic may be controlled by a person with a sign or flag to tell you which direction to travel or to slow down or stop. You must follow their instructions.

Barriers such as drums, cones, and tubes (panels), are used to keep traffic out of hazardous work zones. Along with signs and road markings,   they help guide you safely through a work zone. Barriers may be used to keep drivers from entering closed roads or other areas where it is dangerous to drive. Temporary traffic signals may be used in work zones. You may see a warning sign showing a symbol of a traffic signal. Stop at the white line, if it is present.

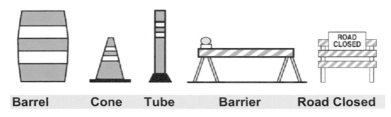

| Barrel | Cone | Tube | Barrier | Road Closed |

Give construction workers a "brake." Reduce your speed in work zones and be prepared to stop suddenly. Do not tailgate in work zones. If you endanger a highway worker you may be fined and have points assessed against your driving record.

SC Code Section 56-5-1535

Regulatory Signs—These signs are square or rectangular or have a special shape and are white with black, red, or green letters or symbols. These signs tell you about specific laws that you must obey, such as rules for traffic direction, lane use, turning, speed, parking, and other special situations. Some regulatory signs have a red circle with a red slash over a symbol, which prohibit certain actions.

Common types of regulatory signs are:

Speed Limit Signs—These black and white signs indicate the maximum legal speed allowed **in ideal conditions**.

Stop Sign—A stop sign has eight sides and is red with white letters. You must stop behind the stop line or crosswalk, if one is present. If a stop line is not present, then stop at the point nearest the intersection where you (the driver) can see in both directions without entering the cross traffic lane. Look for crossing vehicles and pedestrians in all directions and yield the right-of-way.

Yield Sign—A yield sign is a red and white downward-pointing triangle with red letters. It means you must slow down and allow traffic that has the right-of-way to cross before entering.

Shared Center Lane Left Turn Only—This sign tells you where a lane is reserved for the use of left turning vehicles from either direction and is not to be used for through traffic or passing other vehicles.

One-Way Street—These signs tell you that traffic flows only in the direction of the arrow. Do not turn in the opposite direction of the arrow. Never drive the wrong way on a one-way street.

Guide Signs—These signs are square or rectangular and are green, brown, or blue. They give information on intersecting roads, help direct you to cities and towns, and show points of interest along the highway. Guide signs can also help you find hospitals, service stations, restaurants, and hotels.

Route Number Signs—The shape and color of route number signs indicate the type of roadway: interstate, US, state, city, county, or local road. When planning a trip, use a road map to determine the route. During the trip, follow the route signs to prevent getting lost in an unfamiliar area.

Secondary System Road Marker
This sign is a marker used to designate a state secondary system route. The first number after the letter "S" is the number of the county the road is in and the last number is the road number.

There is a separate set of secondary road numbers for each county. You will find only a few of the more important secondary road numbers on a state primary system map because there are too many secondary roads to show. However, they are all shown on county maps, which may be purchased by mail from the central office of the Department of Transportation.

Secondary system roads are local roads built to serve traffic in both rural and urban areas. In rural areas they are not intended as through routes and should not normally be used by drivers who are not familiar with the area.

***Evacuation Route Sign*—** In the event of a hurricane, a mandatory evacuation may be declared for the coastal areas of SC. This sign indicates the road or highway is used as an evacuation route in this type of emergency

Pavement Markings

Pavement markings are lines, arrows, words, or symbols painted on the roadway to give directions or warnings. They are used to divide lanes, tell you when you may pass other vehicles or change lanes, tell you which lanes to use for turns, define pedestrian walkways, and show where you must stop for signs or traffic signals.

Yellow Lane Markings

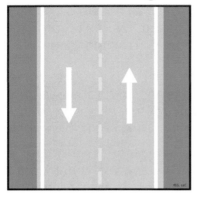

Two-direction roadway—
passing permitted

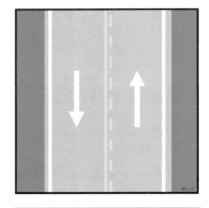

Two-direction roadway—
passing permitted when
dashed line is on your side

Two-direction roadway—
passing prohibited in both
directions

White Lane Markings

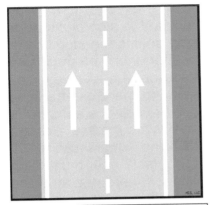

**One-direction roadway—
passing permitted**

Other Lane Controls

Shared Center Left Turn Lane

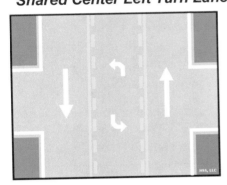

Reversible Lanes

Crosswalks and Stop Lines

Crosswalks define the area where pedestrians may cross the roadway. When required to stop because of a sign or signal you must stop behind the stop line or crosswalk, but if there are neither, then you must stop at the point nearest the intersection where you can see in both directions without entering the cross traffic in front of you. You must yield to pedestrians entering or in a crosswalk. Not all crosswalks are marked. Be alert for pedestrians when crossing intersections. If crosswalks are not apparent, then you must stop before entering the intersection. If there is a stop line before the crosswalk, the stop line must be obeyed first.

Three Common Types of Crosswalk Markings

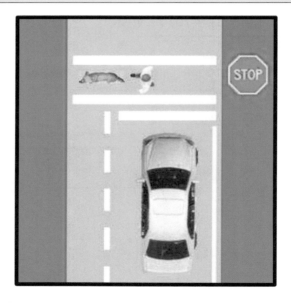

Section 7
General Driving

Turning and Turnabouts

When turning, you should:

- Search all corners for traffic controls, pedestrians, other vehicles, and signal your intentions.

- Enter and maintain in the lane that is closest to the direction you want to go.

- Look through the turn to the farthest point possible along the intended path.

- Accelerate smoothly to appropriate speed, make sure your turn signal is cancelled, and be aware of traffic to the rear.

Right turns

- Avoid swinging wide to the left before making the turn.

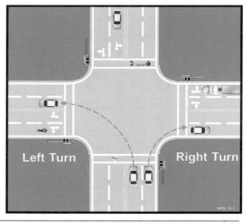

- Always turn right from the right-most portion of your lane.

Left turns

- When making a left turn, yield to oncoming traffic.
- Always turn left from the left-most portion of your lane.

Multiple lanes turning

- Identify and enter the lane from which you will turn.
- Stay in that lane until the turn is completed.

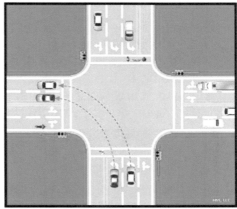

Three-Point Turnabout—Use this type of turnabout only when the road or street is too narrow to make a U-turn and you cannot go around the block. This type of turn should only be used on a two-lane roadway that is not busy. It is better to circle an entire city block if the street is busy.

The three-point turn must be performed without hitting the curb, driving off the road surface, or using a side street or driveway. To perform a three-point turnabout:

1. Check the mirrors and activate your right turn signal to communicate your intention to pull to the right edge of the road. Stop on the right edge of the road.

2. Activate your left turn signal, check traffic, and check blind spot by looking over your left shoulder. When traffic is clear, turn hard left to the other side of the road and stop when you have reached the other side.

3. Place the vehicle in reverse, check traffic, and check blind spots on both sides by looking over your shoulders. Do not depend on your rearview mirror alone. When traffic is clear, turn hard right to the other side of the road and stop.

4. Place the vehicle in drive, and check traffic and blind spots. When traffic is clear, turn hard left and drive forward into the right lane of traffic heading in the new direction. Check traffic and make sure your turn signal has cancelled. Continue driving straight in the new direction.

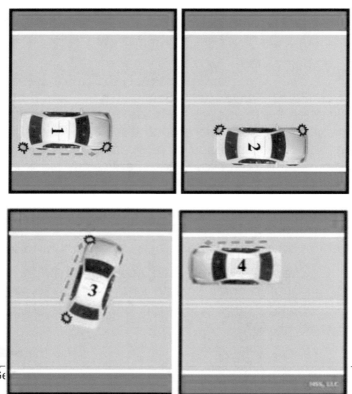

Intersections

At all intersections, reduce your speed and search for:
- traffic control devices,
- oncoming and cross traffic,
- pedestrians and bicyclists,
- the roadway condition, and
- areas of limited visibility.

Do not rely on other road users to obey traffic control signals or signs. You can only control your own driving, but not the driving of others. Some road users may not yield the right-of-way. Be prepared to avoid a collision.

Before moving again after you have stopped at an intersection, take extra time to check for crossing traffic and bicyclists. **You should always look left, then right, and left again before entering the intersection.** At a traffic signal when the light turns green, avoid immediately moving into the intersection. Take time to make sure your path of travel is clear and there is no crossing traffic. You need a large enough gap to get your vehicle across the roadway or to turn into the appropriate lane and accelerate to an appropriate speed.

Never assume another driver will share space with your vehicle or give your vehicle any additional space. Do not turn into a lane just because an approaching vehicle has a turn signal active. The driver with an active turn signal may plan to turn after they go past your vehicle or may have forgotten to turn the signal off from a prior turn.

Diverging Diamond Interchange (DDI)
The primary difference between a DDI and a conventional interchange is the design of the directional crossovers on either side of the interchange. This eliminates the need for left-turning

vehicles to cross the paths of approaching through vehicles. By shifting cross street traffic to the left side of the street between the signalized crossover intersections, vehicles on the crossroad making a left turn on to or off of ramps do not conflict with vehicles approaching from other directions. The DDI design has shown to improve the operations of turning movements to and from the interstate and to significantly reduce the number of vehicle-to-vehicle conflict points compared to a conventional diamond interchange. The DDI also reduces the severity of conflicts.

Restricted Crossing U-turn (RCUT)

The RCUT intersection differs from a conventional intersection by eliminating the left-turn and through movements from cross street approaches. To accommodate these movements, the RCUT intersection requires drivers to turn right onto the main road and then make a u-turn maneuver at a one-way median opening (shown as the red movement in this figure). RCUTs may be controlled by a traffic signal, stop sign, merge- or yield-sign. RCUT intersections reduce potential conflict points and increase safety.

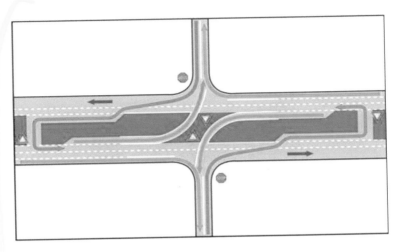

Roundabouts and Traffic Circles

A roundabout, also known as a traffic circle, is a circular intersection with design features that promote safe and efficient traffic flow. Vehicles travel counterclockwise around a raised center island with entering traffic yielding the right-of-way to circulating traffic. When using roundabouts or traffic circles:

- Slow down to enter the roundabout or traffic circle. A sign, like the one shown, warns of a roundabout or traffic circle.

- Yield to the traffic in the roundabout or circle.

- Enter a roundabout or traffic circle in a counterclockwise direction.

- Proceed to the appropriate exit, signal intent, and exit.

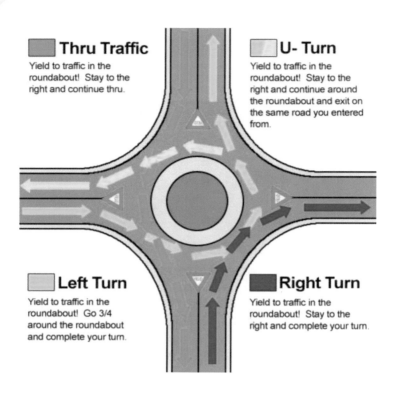

Thru Traffic

Yield to traffic in the roundabout! Stay to the right and continue thru.

U- Turn

Yield to traffic in the roundabout! Stay to the right and continue around the roundabout and exit on the same road you entered from.

Left Turn

Yield to traffic in the roundabout! Go 3/4 around the roundabout and complete your turn.

Right Turn

Yield to traffic in the roundabout! Stay to the right and complete your turn.

Safety Comparison Between Traditional Intersections and Roundabouts

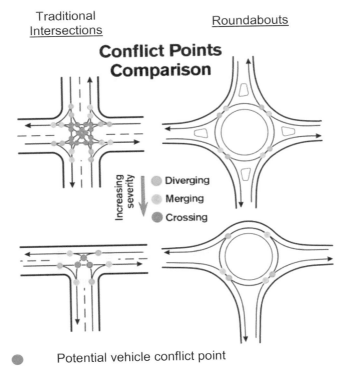

Potential vehicle conflict point

Roundabouts are safer than traditional intersections because they eliminate head-on and high-speed right angle collisions.

Rules for School Buses

You must stop for the entire time a school bus is stopped or preparing to stop with its red or amber lights flashing or its stop arm extended. After the school bus's red and/or amber lights have stopped flashing and the stop arm is no longer visible, proceed slowly, watching for children. Law requires these actions whether you are meeting the school bus or traveling behind it under the following conditions:

- On any two-lane highway
- On any four-lane or multi-lane highway only when traveling behind a school bus
- When attempting to pass a school bus that has red or amber signals flashing

IN **SOUTH CAROLINA**, DO YOU KNOW WHEN TO...
STOP FOR A SCHOOL BUS?

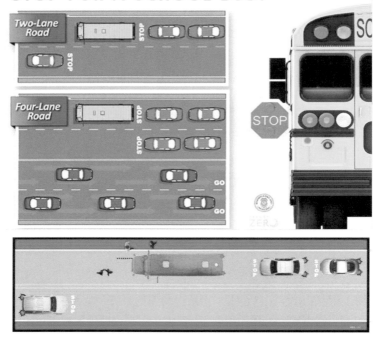

You are required to stop for a stopped school bus when driving on a two-lane road.

You do not have to stop around a school bus in the following circumstances:

1) When the school bus is in a passenger loading zone completely off the main travel lanes and when pedestrians are not allowed to cross the roadway.

2) A driver of a vehicle does not have to stop upon meeting a stopped school bus when traveling in the opposite direction on a multi-lane highway or multi-lane private road. A multi-lane highway or multi-lane private road is defined as a highway or private road that consists of four lanes, having at least two traffic lanes in each direction.

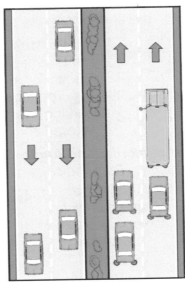

You must always stop on any highway when you are behind the bus. When you have stopped, you must not proceed until the school bus moves or the red lights are no longer flashing. *SC Code Section 56-5-2760*

Parking

You are responsible for making sure that your vehicle is not an obstruction when it is parked. Vehicles displaying a disability license plate or placard may park in designated spaces for people with disabilities, but only if that vehicle is driven by or transporting the person with the disability whose name is on the license plate registration or placard registration certificate.

- Always park in a designated parking area.
- When parking along the roadway, park your vehicle as far away from the flow of traffic as

possible. Do not park more than 18 inches from the curb or edge of pavement.

No-Parking Zones—There are many areas where parking is not allowed. Check for signs or painted curbs that may prohibit or limit parking. Some parking restrictions are indicated by colored curb markings.

Perpendicular and Angle Parking
Entering a Perpendicular or Angle Parking Space

1) Identify the space in which you will park and check traffic.

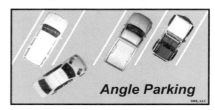

Angle Parking

2) Signal your intentions.

3) Move forward slowly, turning the steering wheel left or right as appropriate, until the vehicle

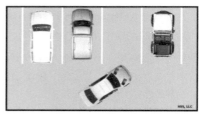

Perpendicular Parking

reaches the middle of the space.

4) Center the vehicle in the space.

5) Move to the front of the parking space, stop, and secure the vehicle.

Exiting a Perpendicular or Angle Parking Space

1) Check for traffic in all directions.

2) Continue to check traffic and move straight back until your front bumper clears the vehicle parked beside you.

3) Then turn the steering wheel sharply in the direction that the rear of your vehicle should move.
4) When the vehicle clears the parking area space, stop and shift to drive.
5) Accelerate smoothly, steering as needed to straighten wheels.

Parallel Parking
Entering a Parallel Parking Space
1) Identify the space where you will park, check traffic, and signal.
2) When traffic is clear, shift to reverse and look to the rear in the direction the vehicle will be moving.
3) Back slowly while turning the steering wheel rapidly in the appropriate direction. Continue backing up until your front bumper is in line with the rear bumper of the vehicle you are parking behind.
4) Back up slowly while turning the steering wheel rapidly to center the vehicle into the space.

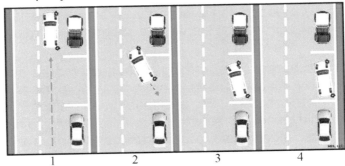

5) Stop before touching the bumper of the vehicle to the rear. Shift to drive and adjust the vehicle in the parking space. Do not park more than 18 inches from the curb or edge of pavement.

Exiting a Parallel Parking Space
1) Check traffic in all directions, place your foot on the brake, shift to reverse, and back up as much as possible to the vehicle parked behind you.
2) Signal and use your mirrors and look over your shoulder to check traffic. Shift to drive and move forward slowly, steering into the lane.
3) Make sure the front bumper of the vehicle will clear the vehicle ahead; if not, reverse and correct steering.
4) Move forward into the appropriate lane of traffic when the door of the vehicle clears the rear bumper of the vehicle parked ahead of you.

Parking on Hills

When parking on hills, you should do the following:
1) Headed downhill, with or without curb: turn wheels to the right (except when parking left on a one way- street).
2) Headed uphill, with curb: turn wheels to the center of the street with the back of the front tire against the curb.
3) Headed uphill, without a curb: turn wheels to the right so that the vehicle will roll off the road if the brakes fail.

In each case, the parking brakes should be set, the vehicle placed in the proper gear or park and the engine turned off. For a manual transmission, the car should be set in first or reverse. When leaving a parking space, signal, use your mirrors and look over your shoulder to check traffic. Yield right of way.

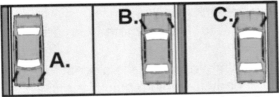

A. Downhill with or without a curve, turn wheels toward curb.
B. Uphill with curb, turn wheels away from curb.
C. Uphill without curb, turn wheels to the right.

Changing Lanes

When changing lanes:

- Check your mirrors.
- Check your "blind spots," or areas around your vehicle that cannot be seen by other vehicles. This is done by turning your head and looking over your shoulder in the direction you plan to move.
- Identify a gap in traffic, signal, and look again in the direction of the lane change. Adjust speed and steer into lane.

Entering a Multi-lane Highway

Use the acceleration lane to reach the speed of other vehicles before pulling onto the roadway. This is the lane that runs alongside the main roadway. Identify a gap in traffic and merge with the traffic flow. Cancel your turn signal.

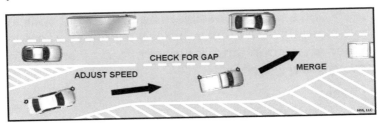

Exiting a Roadway

It is important to know where you are exiting the roadway.

- Plan to move to the lane closest to your existing point early to avoid a quick lane change.
- Maintain your vehicle speed as long as you are on the main roadway.
- Signal your intention, move to the deceleration lane, check for the posted speed, and adjust your speed accordingly. The deceleration lane is to the right of the roadway and before you reach the ramp.

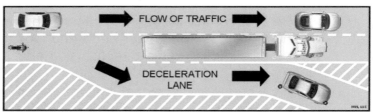

Passing

On multi-lane roads, the left-most lane is to be used for passing slower vehicles. Never pass on the shoulder, whether it is paved or not. The shoulder is a hard surface on the right side of the roadway that is to be used as an emergency stopping lane and not for through traffic.

When passing another vehicle, pass the vehicle as quickly and safely as possible. The longer your vehicle stays alongside the other vehicle, the longer you are in danger of being in the blind spot of the other vehicle moving toward your lane.

To pass:

- Check for oncoming traffic.
- **Check your mirrors and over your shoulder for following or passing vehicles.**

- When it is safe to pass, signal your intentions 100 feet or more before passing.
- Steer smoothly into the passing lane.
- Maintain or adjust speed as necessary.
- Continue to pass until the complete front of the passed vehicle is visible in your rearview mirror.
- Signal your intention to return to the lane. Check traffic over your shoulder for following or passing vehicles.
- Steer smoothly into the lane, maintaining or adjusting speed as appropriate.

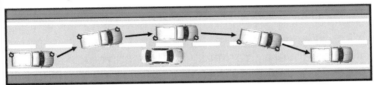

When being passed:
- Stay in your lane.
- Maintain a constant speed to allow the driver to pass you.
- Be on guard so that you may protect yourself from any other driver's potentially unsafe actions.

Do not attempt to pass when an oncoming vehicle is approaching, when your view is blocked by a curve or a hill, while at intersections, or before a highway-railroad crossing or bridge.

Slow down when passing a bicyclist, allow as much space as possible between your vehicle and the bicyclist and consider the bicyclist's speed when you pass.

Zipper Merge (Late Merge)

The Zipper Merge is a new driving strategy that requires a change in the way of thinking of drivers who were taught to merge early when noticing that a lane will end. Merging early can lead to unexpected and dangerous lane switching, collisions, and road rage.

Zipper merging reduces these dangers by using both lanes until reaching the merge area. When you see a "lane closed ahead" sign **and traffic is backing up**, stay in your current lane of traffic until you reach the point of merge. Then take turns with the other drivers to, safely and smoothly, ease into the open lane of traffic. **When traffic is heavy and slow**, it is much safer for drivers to remain in their current traffic lane until the point where drivers can take turns merging into the open lane of traffic.

Law does not require the Zipper Merge to be used, but it is a best practice especially when a lane is closed in a construction zone. The Zipper Merge benefits drivers by:

- Reducing the difference in speeds between two lanes. Changing lanes when traffic is traveling at approximately the same speed is easier and safer.

- Reducing the overall length of traffic backup by as much as 40%.

- Reducing congestion on the interstate.
- Creating a sense of fairness and equity that all lanes are moving at the same rate.
- Reducing incidents of road rage.

When not to use the zipper merge

When traffic is moving at highway speeds and there are no backups, it makes sense to move sooner to the lane that will remain open. The bottom line is to **merge when it is safe to do so**.

Section 8
Safe Driving Tips

This Section Covers
- Visual Search
- Speed Management
- Stopping Distance
- Space Management
- Communicating

Driving requires skills you can only gain through practice and experience. The following section offers driving tips you can practice to help you become a safer and more skillful driver.

Visual Search

You must know what is happening around your vehicle before you start a vehicle and while driving. You must look ahead, to the sides, and behind the vehicle. You should develop a searching pattern and use it every time you drive.

Searching helps you see situations that could cause a problem and gives you time to change your actions such as speed or roadway position. Avoid staring at any one thing. Keep your eyes moving and searching for possible problems.

Look ahead. Looking well down your planned path of travel will help you see the road, other road users, and traffic conditions which allows you time to adjust and plan your driving movements. This additional time will allow you to make better decisions and possibly avoid being forced to use emergency braking and steering. Ideally, you should try to look at what is occurring 20 to 30 seconds in front of your vehicle.

How far you look down the road depends on where you are driving. In cities and urban areas, you may not be able to see as far as when you are driving on a highway. Avoid getting into situations that could limit how far you can see such as following too close to a larger vehicle. Adjust your speed and road position so you can best see.

Look to the sides. It is important to search the sides of your vehicle to see if other roadway users are about to cross your travel path.

Look to the rear. It is also important to be aware of traffic behind your vehicle, especially when changing lanes, slowing down or stopping, or entering an intersection. Use your mirrors to check this traffic.

Speed Management

Driving safely means adjusting your vehicle speed for roadway and traffic conditions, providing an adequate following distance, and obeying the appropriate speed limits.

Adjusting To Roadway Conditions

Curves—Always reduce speed before entering a curve to a safe speed (a speed that allows you to apply slight and constant acceleration through the curve). Reduce speed more when traction is poor, when following other vehicles, and when you cannot see the end of the curve. Hard braking after entry to a curve could cause the vehicle tires to lose traction.

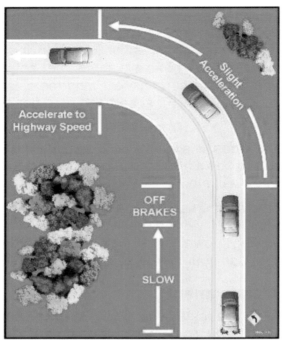

Slippery roads—Reduce speed at the first sign of rain, snow, sleet, or ice. When the roadway is slippery tires do not grip as well. It will take longer to stop and will be harder to turn without skidding. Always reduce your speed if the road is wet or covered with snow or ice.

Hydroplaning—Hydroplaning occurs when the steering tires ride on a layer of water on top of the road surface, similar to the action of water skis. The best way to avoid traction loss from hydroplaning is to slow down when driving in the rain or on a road that is wet with pooled water or water puddles.

Flooded roadways—If you see a flooded roadway or barricades blocking a flooded roadway, find another route to get to your destination. Flooding can occur when rivers and streams overflow their banks, when dams or levees break, when there is run-off from deep snow or any time there is heavy rainfall. Floodwaters can be found on roads, bridges and low areas. Flash floods can come rapidly and unexpectedly. They can occur within a few minutes or hours of excessive rainfall.

- Do not drive through flooded areas. If you see a flooded roadway ahead, turn around and find another route to get to your destination.

- Be cautious, especially at night, when the visibility is limited.

- Remember, six inches of water will reach the bottom of most passenger cars, causing loss of control or possible stalling. Two feet of moving water can carry away most vehicles, including sport utility vehicles and pick-up trucks.

- Even if the water appears shallow enough to cross, do not attempt to cross a flooded road. Water can hide dips and other unseen hazards. Floodwaters can also damage roadways by washing away the underlying road surface.

- If there is no other route, proceed to higher ground and wait for the water to subside.

Stopping Distance

Total stopping distance is the distance your vehicle travels, in ideal conditions, from the time you realize you must stop until your vehicle actually stops. Several things may affect your stopping distance:

- Speed—The faster you are traveling, the more time and distance is needed to stop.

- Your perception time—This is the time and distance it takes you to recognize you must stop. The average perception time for an alert driver is ¾ second to 1 second.

- Your reaction time—This is the time and distance it takes for you to react by moving your foot from the gas pedal and beginning to apply the brakes. The average driver has a reaction time of ¾ second to 1 second.

- Braking distance—This is the time and distance it takes for your brakes to slow and stop your vehicle. At 50 mph on dry pavement with good brakes, it can take about 158 feet.

Space Management

Providing an Adequate Following Distance

You will share the road with different type of vehicles (cars, trucks, motorcycles, etc.). You will need time and space to adjust and react to these other road users. The more space you allow between your vehicle and other roadway users, the more time you have to react. This space is usually referred to as a space cushion. Always try to maintain a safe space cushion around your vehicle.

Space in Front

Following a vehicle in front of you too closely limits your vision of the road and does not allow you enough time to react to avoid a collision. You should always try to keep a minimum following distance of 4 seconds between your vehicle and the vehicle in front.

To determine your following distance:

1) Watch when the rear of the vehicle ahead passes a sign, pole, or any other stationary point.

2) Count the seconds it takes you to reach the same sign, pole, or any other stationary point ("One thousand one, one thousand two, one thousand three, one thousand four").

3) You are following too closely if you pass the stationary point before counting to "one thousand four".

4) Reduce speed and then count again at another stationary point to check the new following distance. Repeat until you are following no closer than 4 seconds.

To check your accuracy in maintaining a minimum following distance of 4 seconds you may guess how many seconds away you are from an object and then count the seconds it takes to reach the object.

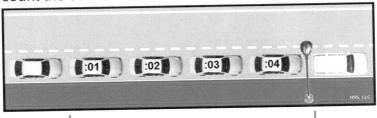

4 Second Minimum Following Distance

There are certain situations when you need more space in front of your vehicle. Increase your following distance:

- On slippery roads

- At night, in fog, or in inclement weather

- When following vehicles required to stop at railroad crossings, such as transit buses, school buses, or vehicles carrying hazardous materials

- When following large vehicles such as trucks, buses, recreational vehicles, and vehicles pulling a trailer

Space to the Side

A space cushion on the sides of your vehicle allows you to move right or left.

- Avoid driving next to other vehicles for long periods of time. You may be in their blind spot and this reduces the space you may need to avoid a collision.

- Avoid crowding the centerline marking. Try to keep as much space as possible between you and oncoming traffic.

- Make space for vehicles entering a multiple-lane or limited access roadway by moving over a lane or adjusting your speed.

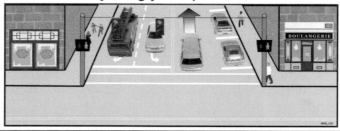

- Give extra space to pedestrians, especially children, the elderly, and bicyclists.
- When a passing vehicle is a tractor trailer, leave a little more space by moving to the outside portion of your lane space away from the tractor trailer as it passes.

Space Behind Affects Your Following Distance

It is not always easy to maintain a safe following distance behind your vehicle. However, you can help keep the driver in the vehicle behind you at a safe distance by keeping a steady speed, signaling in advance, and keeping more space to the front of your vehicle before you reduce speed or turn.

Communicating

It is important that you let other roadway users know where you are and what you plan to do.

Letting Others Know You Are There

It is your responsibility to make your vehicle is visible to other roadway users.

Use headlights—Turning on your headlights helps other roadway users see you.

This is especially important:

- On rainy, snowy, or foggy days; use your low-beam lights and slow down
- When it begins to get dark or when driving away from a rising or setting sun

Using your horn—Your vehicle's horn, if used properly, can get the attention of other road users. A light tap on the horn should be all that is needed under normal circumstances. You may want to give your horn a light tap when:

- Pedestrians or bicyclists appear to be moving into your lane of travel

- Passing a driver who starts to turn into your lane

- A driver is not paying attention or may have trouble seeing you

Not using your horn—You should only use your horn when you need to communicate with other road users. Using your horn inappropriately could scare or anger another road user. You should not use your horn when near blind pedestrians.

Signaling Your Movements

Using the appropriate turn signal before changing direction or slowing your vehicle informs and warns other roadway users.

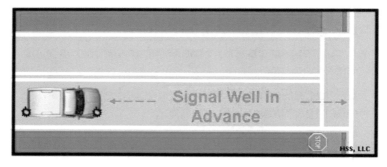

Signal Well in Advance

HSS, LLC

Signal before changing direction—An appropriate signal gives other roadway users time to react to your vehicle movements. It is state law that you must use a turn signal 100 feet or more before changing lanes, turning left or right, or when merging into traffic. Make sure you cancel your signals once your action is completed to avoid confusing other drivers.

Signal when reducing speeds—Brake lights let other roadway users know that the vehicle in front is slowing down. Signal before reducing speed when:

- Turning off a roadway that does not have separate turning or exiting lanes
- Parking or turning before an intersection

Section 9

Emergency Situations and Avoiding Collisions

Emergencies and Avoiding Collisions

Most drivers will eventually find themselves in an emergency situation. As careful as you are, there are situations that could cause a problem for you. If you are prepared, you may be able to prevent any serious outcomes. All drivers have the responsibility to do all they can to prevent collisions. You have three options to avoid a collision or to reduce its impact. These options are braking, steering, or accelerating.

Braking

The first reaction for most drivers to avoid a collision is to stop the vehicle. Most new vehicles are equipped with an anti-lock braking system (ABS). The ABS will allow you to stop your vehicle without skidding and keep steering control. Be sure to read the vehicle owner's manual on how to use the ABS. The ABS system will allow you to stop without skidding. The general guidelines for using ABS are:

- Press on the brake pedal as hard as you can and keep applying constant pressure. Do **not** pump the brakes because this will deactivate ABS.

- ABS will work only if you keep the pressure on the brake pedal. You may feel the pedal vibrate and you may hear a clicking noise. This is normal.

- You can still steer you vehicle while ABS is activated.

If your vehicle is not equipped with ABS, refer to your vehicle owner's manual for proper braking procedure.

Steering

You may be able to avoid a collision by quickly steering around a problem. This is sometimes referred to as swerving. To quickly steer around a problem:

- Make sure you have a good grip with both hands on the steering wheel.
- Steer in the direction you want to go but try to avoid other traffic.
- When you have cleared the problem, steer in the opposite direction to straighten out your vehicle, gain control, and adjust to an appropriate driving speed.

Accelerating

It may be necessary to accelerate to avoid a collision. This may happen when another vehicle is about to hit you from behind or the side.

Dealing with Skids

Skids are caused when you are traveling too fast for the road conditions, when you stop suddenly, or when the tires can no longer grip the roadway. When you begin to skid, you have little control of your vehicle. If your vehicle begins to skid:

- Release pressure from the brake or accelerator.
- Look where you want to go and steer the vehicle in the direction you want to go.

Uneven Surface Drop-Offs

Uneven surface drop-offs can cause serious collisions if you react improperly. Avoid panic steering which means when someone tries to return to the pavement as soon as the vehicle wheels leave the pavement. If your vehicle leaves the paved road surface due to an uneven surface drop-off, slow down gradually when safe to do so, and steer gently back onto the pavement. The key to safely driving off the road and safely returning involves gradually moving off and back on the road. The turning of the steering wheel should be slight. This reduces the chance of erratic vehicle behavior when your tires encounter an uneven or unpaved shoulder.

Vehicle Malfunctions

There is always a chance of a vehicle problem while driving. It is important to follow the recommended maintenance schedule listed in the vehicle owner's manual. The following preventive maintenance measures greatly reduces the chance that your vehicle will have a problem.

Brake Failure

It is important to check all of your warning lights, including the brake light, to be sure your vehicle is working correctly. A brake warning light will tell you if your brakes are not working properly. Do not drive if you see this warning light. In the event your brakes stop working while driving:

- Use the parking brake. Pull on the parking brake handle in the center console or push the parking brake foot pedal slowly so you will not lock the rear wheels and cause a skid. Be ready to release the parking brake if the vehicle does start to skid.

- If the parking brake does not work, turn off the engine and look for a safe place to slow to a stop. Make sure the vehicle is off the roadway. Do not continue to drive the vehicle without working brakes.

Tire Blowout

A tire blowout is a rapid deflation of air from a tire. If a front tire blows out, the vehicle will pull sharply in the direction of the blowout. If a rear tire blows out, the vehicle will wobble, shake, and pull some in the direction of the blowout. If a tire blows out or suddenly goes flat:

1) Grip the steering wheel firmly and keep the vehicle going straight.

2) Slow down gradually. Take your foot off the accelerator pedal.

3) Do not brake. Allow the vehicle to slow by itself or brake gently if necessary.

4) Do not stop on the road if at all possible. Pull off the road in a safe place and turn on emergency flashers.

5) Have the tire changed and replaced.

Power Failure

If the engine shuts off while you are driving:

1) Keep a strong grip on the steering wheel. Be aware that the steering wheel may be difficult to turn, but it is still able to be turned.

2) Look for an escape path. Do not brake hard; instead, brake with steady pressure on the pedal, slow down, and then pull off the roadway.

3) Stop and try to restart the engine; if unsuccessful, raise the hood and turn on the emergency flashers. Call for help.

Stuck Accelerator

If your vehicle is accelerating out of control, you should:

1) Turn off the engine.

2) Shift to neutral and search for an escape path.

3) Steer smoothly, brake gently, and pull off the roadway.

4) Have the pedal repaired at a service center before driving again.

Vehicle Breakdown

If your vehicle breaks down on the highway, you should make sure that other roadway users can see your disabled vehicle. All too often, collisions occur because a driver did not see a disabled vehicle until it was too late to stop.

If available, use your cell phone or other device to notify authorities that your vehicle or another vehicle has broken down. If you are having vehicle trouble and have to stop:

- Get your vehicle off the road and away from traffic, if possible.

- Turn on your emergency flashers to show your vehicle is disabled.

- Try to warn other roadway users that your vehicle is there. If you have emergency flares, place them about 200 to 300 feet behind the vehicle, giving other drivers some time to change lanes if necessary.

Emergency Contact Information

If you hold a beginner's permit, driver's license, or identification card, please enter your emergency contact information on your SCDMV record through SCDMV's website at www.scdmvonline.com. If you are ever in a collision or have a medical emergency, SC law enforcement officers will then have access to your emergency contact information and may provide it to medical personnel.

Section 10
Sharing the Road

This Section Covers
- Pedestrians
- Bicyclists
- Motorcyclists
- Interacting with Commercial Vehicles
- Emergency Vehicles
- What to Do and Expect When Stopped by Law Enforcement
- Move-Over Law
- Slow-Moving Vehicles

Remember to be courteous and communicate your presence and intentions to others on the roadway to avoid collisions.

Pedestrians

Pedestrians are difficult to see and it is difficult to determine their intentions. As a driver:

- Always be prepared to yield to pedestrians even if they are not in a crosswalk.

- You must yield when a pedestrian is in a crosswalk, even if it is unmarked, including mid-block crosswalks marked by warning signs and pavement markings.

- You must always yield the right-of-way to persons who are visually impaired. When a pedestrian is crossing a street guided by a dog or carrying a white cane, you must come to a complete stop.

- You must yield the right-of-way to all pedestrians in the intersection even if the traffic light is green.

- When making a right or left turn on red, you must be prepared to yield the right-of-way to pedestrians.

- When driving next to parked or stopped vehicles, pedestrians can walk out between these vehicles. Slow down and do not pass until you are sure there are no pedestrians crossing in front of it.

- Check for pedestrians in your path before backing up, especially in parking lots or places where there are many pedestrians.

- Be careful in playground and residential areas where children could run out from between parked vehicles. It is a good idea to drive slower than the speed limit in these areas and be prepared to stop quickly.

- In a school zone when lights are flashing or children are present, you must obey a slower speed limit. At a school crossing where there is traffic patrol, stop and yield if you are signaled to do so.

Bicyclists

Bicycles are considered vehicles when on roadways. Bicyclists are required and expected to follow the same rules of the road as motorized vehicles. As a motorist, you should know that a bicyclist has the same rights, privileges, and responsibilities as you. Respect for each other will aid in the smooth flow of traffic.

Bicyclists may not be easily seen in traffic. You must to be alert for bicyclists and be extra careful when approaching them. Just as motorists have different levels of skills, bicyclists also have varying levels of skills. A skillful bicyclist rides predictably and holds a steady line. An unskillful bicyclist may swerve unpredictably, ignore traffic signs and signals, and ride without a light at night. If you see an unskillful bicyclist, be ready for any sudden movements.

As a driver:

- Yield to bicyclists in intersections as you would for pedestrians and other vehicles.

- Yield right-of-way when a bicycle path or bike lane intersects a road. Do not stop, park, or drive on a designated bicycle path or lane unless you are entering or leaving an alley or driveway, performing official duties, directed by a police officer, or if an emergency situation exists.

- Allow as much space as possible and slow down when approaching or passing a bicyclist. You should slow down and let the cyclist clear the intersection before making your turn.

- Avoid slowing down or stopping quickly. A motor vehicle's brakes are more powerful than a bicycle's and you could cause a collision.

- Avoid sounding your horn close to bicyclists unless there is a chance of a collision. Sounding your horn to alert your presence may startle bicyclists and cause them to steer into your path resulting in a collision.

- Watch carefully for bicyclists entering your lane. Be especially careful if you see children riding bikes on the sidewalk. They may come onto the road.
- Avoid turning sharply in front of a bicyclist and do not force a bicyclist off the road.
- Although bicyclists are required to ride in the direction of traffic, you should look for them riding anywhere on the roadway.
- Be particularly careful around bicyclists when the roadway is wet or covered with sand or gravel. These conditions affect bicycles much more than vehicles.
- Cooperate with bicyclists. They are required to use hand signals, as shown, when turning and stopping. However, keep in mind that bicyclists may not know how to use hand signals or may be unable to signal if road or traffic conditions require them to keep both hands on the handlebars. Look for other clues of a bicyclist's intent, such as turning his or her head or looking over his or her shoulder before changing lane positions.

Stop   **Left Turn**

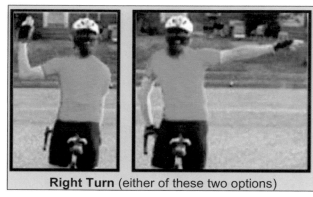

Right Turn (either of these two options)

- When parked on the street, check to the sides and rear of the vehicle for bicyclists before you open your vehicle door.

- You should check for bicyclists in your path before backing up. Be especially cautious near schools or residential areas where bicyclists are more likely to be present.

Motorcyclists

Motorcyclists have the same rights and responsibilities as other drivers. However, it may be more difficult to see them. There are special situations and conditions drivers need to be aware of so the road can be safely shared with motorcyclists:

- Allow a motorcyclist a full lane width. Do not share the lane. The motorcycle needs space for the motorcyclist to react to other traffic.

- Motorcycles are small and therefore more difficult to see. Be aware that motorcycles can be part of the traffic mix. Always check your mirrors and blind spots for them.

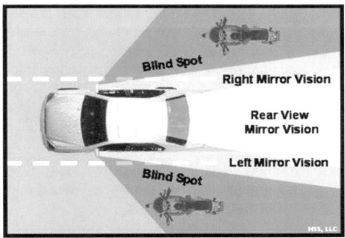

- Before turning left, be alert for motorcycles by looking carefully to the front and sides of your vehicle.

Do not assume anybody is turning When their turn signal is on

- Do not assume a motorcycle is turning when you see its turn signal flashing. Motorcycle turn signals may not self-cancel and the motorcyclist may have forgotten to turn them off. Wait to be sure the rider is going to turn before you proceed.

- When following a motorcyclist allow for a minimum 4 second following distance or more in wet conditions or you may not have enough time or space to avoid a collision. Motorcycle riders may suddenly need to change speed or adjust lane position to avoid hazards such as potholes, gravel, wet or slippery surfaces, pavement seams, railroad crossings, and grooved pavement, which can be deadly to a motorcyclist.

- Keep in mind that scooters and mopeds travel at much slower speeds than motorcycles.

Interacting with Commercial Vehicles

More than 250,000 collisions occur between cars and commercial vehicles each year. Many of these collisions could be avoided by keeping these points in mind:

- Commercial vehicles are generally larger vehicles and less easily maneuverable than cars.

- These vehicles have much larger blind spots than cars.

- They have longer stopping and accelerating distances and need more room to turn.

The No Zone

The no zone is the area around commercial vehicles such as large trucks or buses where vehicles  disappear from the commercial driver's view into blind spots. These blind spots are located on the sides, rear, and front commercial vehicles.

- *Side No Zones*—Large trucks and buses have big no zones on both sides. They are much larger than a regular vehicle's blind spots. Trucks have a larger blind spot on their right side starting behind the cab and extending up to the length of the truck. **If you cannot see the driver's face in the side view mirror, he or she cannot see you.** Avoid driving alongside a large vehicle for any longer than required under all circumstances. If the driver of a large vehicle needs to swerve or change lanes, the chances of a collision are greatly increased.

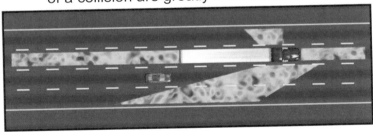

- **Front No Zones**—Because of a large vehicle's size and weight, they take longer to stop than cars. A loaded truck with good tires and properly adjusted brakes, under ideal conditions, traveling at 55 mph, requires a minimum of 335 feet before coming to a complete stop, or greater than 1½ times the stopping distance of a car. Therefore, it is essential not to enter a roadway in front of a large vehicle or change lanes in front of a large vehicle. When passing a large vehicle, look for the whole front of the vehicle in your rear-view mirror before pulling in front and be sure to maintain your speed.

- **Rear No Zones**—Unlike cars, large vehicles have huge blind spots directly behind them that extend up to 200 feet. If you are too close, the large vehicle cannot see your vehicle, and you cannot see what is ahead of you. If the large vehicle brakes or stops suddenly, you have no place to go and could run into the large vehicle. To prevent this, pay close attention when following a large vehicle. Avoid following the vehicle too closely and position your vehicle so the driver can see it in his or her side mirrors. When traveling up or down steep hills, large vehicles must drive slowly, approximately 35 mph, and therefore use the right lane. Avoid driving in the right lane, if possible, when traveling up or down hills, as well as near truck weigh stations, where large vehicles will be attempting to re-enter faster moving traffic. By avoiding the right lane in these areas, you will reduce the possibility of a collision with a large vehicle.

Turning

Pay close attention to large vehicles turn signals and give them plenty of room to maneuver. When a truck or bus needs to make a right turn, the driver will sometimes swing the vehicle wide to the left to safely turn right and clear the corner of a curb or other obstruction. Sometimes space from other lanes is used to clear corners. If you try to get in between the truck or bus and the curb, you will be squeezed in-between the vehicle and could suffer a serious collision. To avoid a collision, do not turn until the truck or bus has completed its turn.

Keep in mind:

- When you meet a truck coming from the opposite direction, keep as far as possible to the right side of the roadway to avoid a side-swept collision and to reduce the wind turbulence between the two vehicles, which pushes the vehicles apart.

- Many collisions with large vehicles occur at intersections because motorists are unable to judge accurately the speed of a truck approaching before making a left turn. When in doubt about the speed of an oncoming truck or bus, do not turn left in its path. The truck or bus may be going faster than you think, and it takes longer for a truck or bus to stop.

- Many intersections are marked with stop lines to show where you must come to a complete stop. These stop lines help to set you farther back at an intersection to give larger vehicles more turning space. Always stop behind stop lines.

- Do not cut off a large vehicle in traffic or on the highway to reach an exit or turn or to beat a truck into a single-lane construction zone. The few seconds that might be saved are not worth a life.

Emergency Vehicles

Emergency vehicles are equipped with sirens, flashing lights, and special horns to help them move more efficiently through traffic.

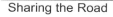

As a driver, you must yield right-of-way to an emergency vehicle when the flashing lights and siren are on by pulling over to the edge of the road so the emergency vehicle(s) may more easily pass. Avoid blocking intersections, roadways, or driveways whenever possible

What to Do and Expect When Stopped by Law Enforcement

A law enforcement officer conducts a traffic stop because she or he observes a traffic violation or is conducting a police investigation. Being stopped by a law enforcement officer can be a stressful experience, but knowing what to do during the stop will help ensure your safety, the safety of other motorists, and the safety of the officer.

When you see emergency lights behind you, <u>stay calm</u>, activate your turn signal, and pull to the side of the roadway as soon and safely as possible. Turn off the ignition and radio, turn on your hazard flashers, and <u>stay in your vehicle unless the officer directs you to exit</u>.

<u>Keep your hands on the steering wheel so they can be easily seen</u>. Ask your passengers to remain calm. Everyone should keep his or her seatbelt fastened and stay in the vehicle while <u>keeping his or her hands in plain view as well</u>. <u>Give the officer your full attention</u>. Cell phones and mobile devices should not be used by you or any of your passengers at this time. Do not make sudden movements or search for your driver's license or vehicle documents. Wait for the officer to give you instructions.

If you have one or more weapon in the vehicle, <u>inform the officer of all weapons upon first contact</u>. Concealed weapons permit (CWP) holders should follow CWP procedures.

If it is nighttime, the officer may direct a spotlight at your vehicle once stopped. To assist with visibility, turn on your interior lights as soon as you stop to help the officer see inside your vehicle.

Roll down the window so that you and the officer can communicate. The officer will usually explain why he or she stopped you and may ask questions about your trip. If the officer is driving an unmarked vehicle or is not in uniform, ask to see his or her law enforcement credentials. Follow all instructions the officer gives you or your passengers. The officer may ask to see your driver's license, proof of insurance, and vehicle registration. <u>If the documents are out of your reach, tell the officer where they are and ask if you may reach for them</u>. If you have questions, politely ask for clarification. If the officer asks you to exit the vehicle, stay safely away from traffic and keep your hands in plain view.

When the officer completes his or her interaction with you, the officer may issue a warning or a traffic ticket, which may include a fine. The officer will typically explain whatever action is being taken. If you have questions, respectfully ask the officer to clarify. If you disagree with the officer's decision to issue a traffic ticket, do not prolong the contact by arguing with the officer. If you wish to contest the ticket, you will have the opportunity to explain your point in court. Your acceptance of a traffic ticket document is not considered an admission of guilt. In SC it is not a requirement that a driver sign a traffic ticket. However, in another state the refusal to sign a traffic ticket may result in your arrest based on the laws of the state in which the traffic ticket is being issued.

If you believe the officer acted inappropriately, report it to the officer's agency in a timely manner. The name of the officer and law enforcement agency will be on the ticket, or you may ask the officer to provide this information.

The enforcement of traffic laws is an effective tool in changing unsafe driving behavior and reducing collisions. If you receive a warning or a ticket for a traffic violation, its purpose is to deter illegal and/or unsafe behavior. Good communication from all involved parties can make a traffic stop a safe experience for all.

If the officer believes a crime has been committed, he or she can search your vehicle without a court-issued warrant as long as the officer has probable cause. Do not make threatening motions or statements to an officer. Keep your emotions under control. Never attempt to interfere with the arrest of others who may be with you. Do not resist arrest for any reason.

Never try to run from law enforcement. It is very dangerous, and many deadly collisions occur from police chases. The consequences of running from law enforcement are more severe than any initial traffic citation.

Move-Over Law

The incidents are increasing of law enforcement officers, emergency medical services, fire department personnel, and tow truck operators being struck while performing duties on the road. To lessen this problem, SC and most other states, have enacted move-over laws, which require drivers to slow down and change lanes when approaching emergency vehicles.

When you approach a stopped authorized emergency vehicle, proceed with caution. Slow down and yield the right-of-way by making a lane change into a lane away from the authorized emergency vehicle, if safety and traffic conditions permit. If a lane change is unsafe, slow down and proceed with caution while maintaining a safe speed for traffic conditions.

When you see these
SLOW DOWN & MOVE OVER
It's the Law
SC Code § 56-5-1538 (2012)

Drive Safely

Slow Down
Move Over

Slow-Moving Vehicles

Be alert for slow-moving vehicles, especially in rural areas. A fluorescent or reflective orange and red triangle displayed on the rear of a vehicle drawn by animals or are farm or construction equipment means the vehicle is traveling less than 25 mph. Use caution when approaching a slow-moving vehicle, and be sure it is safe before you pass.

- **Farm machinery**—Watch for tractors, combines, and other farm equipment moving across roads and traveling on state highways in rural areas. Pass with caution and remember that the operator of farm machinery most likely cannot hear approaching vehicles due to the noise level of the machinery.

- **Animal-drawn vehicles and horseback riders**—In some rural areas, you may be sharing the road with animal-drawn vehicles and horseback riders. They have the same rights to use the road as a motor vehicle and must also follow the same rules of the road. They are subject to heavy damage and injury to their occupants if hit by a vehicle. Pass with caution and do not use your horn or "rev" your vehicle's engine because this may scare the animal and cause a collision. To avoid other possible collisions, be sure to anticipate left turns made by animal-drawn vehicles into fields and driveways. Warning signs may be posted in areas where you are likely to find animal-drawn vehicles and horseback riders, so be alert.

Section 11

Special Driving Situations

This Section Covers
• Night Driving
• Work Zones
• Rural Road Driving
• Winter Driving Techniques

Night Driving

Driving at night is more difficult and hazardous than daytime driving. The distance you can see in front is limited by light provided by your headlights. Here are some things you can do that will help when you are driving at night:

- **Use your high beams whenever there are no oncoming vehicles.** High beams let you see twice as far as low beams.

- Dim your high beams when you are 500 feet or more away from any oncoming vehicle. If a vehicle comes toward you with its high beams on, glance toward the right side of the road to keep from being distracted or momentarily blinded by the vehicle's headlights.

- Use your low beams when following another vehicle that is less than 200 feet in front of you.

- In fog, rain, or snow, use your low beams. Light from your high beams may cause glare and make it more difficult to see ahead. Some vehicles have fog lights that can be used in fog, snow or rain.

- Avoid looking directly into oncoming headlights. Keep your eyes searching the road in front of your vehicle.

- Try to search well ahead of your headlight beams, looking for dark shapes on the roadway.

- Glance occasionally to the right and left to determine the location of the edge of the pavement and any possible hazards that may come from the sides.

- Do not wear sunglasses or colored lenses when driving at night or on overcast days. Tinted or colored lenses reduce your vision.

- Increase your following distance by adding at least one additional second for night driving conditions and at least two additional seconds for driving on unfamiliar roadways at night.

Work Zones

A work zone is an area where roadwork takes place and may involve a lane closure, a detour, and moving equipment.

Work zones have become increasingly dangerous places for both workers and drivers. Approximately 40,000 people per year are injured as a result of motor vehicle collisions in work zones.

When approaching a work zone, watch for signs, cones, barrels, large vehicles, and workers. Work zone signs have orange backgrounds and black

letters or symbols. Always reduce your speed in a work zone, even if there are no workers. The narrower lanes and rough pavement can create hazardous

conditions. If you endanger a highway worker you may be fined and have points assessed against your driving record. *SC Code Section 56-5-1535.*

As a driver in a work zone, you should:

- Reduce your speed, increase your following distance, watch the traffic around you, and be prepared to stop.

- Use extreme caution when driving through a work zone at night **whether workers are present or not**.

- Adjust your lane position to allow space for workers and construction vehicles.

- Observe the posted work zone signs until you see "End Road Work."

- Expect delays, plan for them, and leave earlier to reach your destination.

- When possible, use alternate routes and avoid work zones.

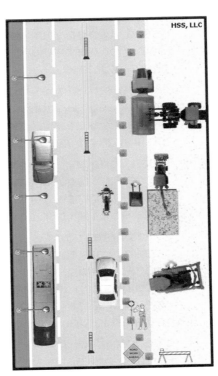

Rural Road Driving

Driving on rural roads can be dangerous. Stay alert, watch for warning signs, and obey the speed limit. Some road conditions and driving hazards are unique to rural roads. It is important to understand the different road conditions you may experience on rural roads:

- *Gravel or dirt*—Traction can be reduced on gravel or dirt roads. You should reduce your speed, increase your following distance, and realize you may skid when trying to stop your vehicle.

- *Narrow roads*—Rural roads are generally narrower and may have ditches or drop- offs instead of shoulders. You should reduce your speed, center your vehicle in your lane, and watch for oncoming traffic that may attempt to share your lane.

- *Narrow and single-lane bridges*—Be aware of warning signs identifying narrow or single-lane bridges. Take turns crossing a bridge; generally, the first driver to the bridge has the right-of-way.

- *Open bridge gratings or steel bridges*— These can reduce your traction. Reduce your speed, increase your following distance, and maintain a firm grip on the steering wheel.

- *Areas of reduced vision*—Blind corners (street corners you cannot see around) created by wooded areas, crops growing in fields, and steep hills can limit how far you can see. In this type of area always reduce your speed and be prepared to stop.

- *Uncontrolled intersections*—Some intersections on rural roads are not controlled by yield or stop signs. These intersections can be very dangerous if they are not approached with caution. When approaching an uncontrolled rural intersection, slow down and be prepared to stop for crossing or oncoming traffic.

Winter Driving Techniques

South Carolina generally does not have extreme winters but occasionally gets some snow and ice. Winter weather conditions call for a different kind of driving than other weather conditions such as slower speeds, slower acceleration, slower steering, and slower braking.

Be especially careful on bridges, overpasses, and infrequently traveled roadways because they tend to freeze first. Even at temperatures above freezing, if the conditions are wet, you might encounter ice in shady areas or on exposed roadways like bridges. Be aware that road conditions are constantly changing.

If you must drive, it is recommended that you use tire chains or special snow tires on your vehicle. Also:

- Keep your windshield and windows clear.

- Use the defroster because it improves driver visibility, especially during cold weather. Activate the fan and place your hand on the dashboard to ensure it is working properly.

- Load extra weight into the trunk of your car. This will help give your car traction (rear wheel drive). Keep a full tank of gasoline to prevent condensation within your gas tank, which may freeze. This will reduce further problems.

- When possible, travel in the tracks where other vehicles have gone before.

- Test road conditions carefully. Applying the brakes gently is best for slowing down or stopping.

- Avoid using cruise control in winter driving conditions.

- Allow additional distance between your vehicle and others when there is snow or ice. (Ice patches may occur on bridges even when there is no ice on the roads.)

- Approach intersections with caution.

- Generally avoid hills, but if necessary, drive slowly and keep a steady pace and a good distance of space between you and the vehicle ahead. If you stop on a hill, it is extremely difficult, if not impossible, to get going again.

- If your vehicle gets stuck in the snow, do not spin your wheels. This will only dig the vehicle in deeper.
  - Turn your wheels from side to side a few times to push snow out of the way.
  - Use a light touch on the gas, to ease your car out.
  - Use a shovel to clear snow away from the wheels and the underside of the car.
  - Pour sand, cat litter, gravel, or salt in the path of the wheels to help get traction. You can also try using cardboard, newspaper, or brush under your wheels.
- If your vehicle starts to skid, take your foot off the accelerator and steer in the direction you want the front of the vehicle to go.
  - If you have ABS, do not pump the brakes. Apply steady pressure to the brakes. You will feel the brakes pulse, which is normal.
  - If you have standard brakes, pump them gently.
- Do not abandon your vehicle in the roadway, if possible.

Section 12
Test Your Knowledge

This Section Covers
• Practice Beginner's Permit Knowledge Test
• Sample Knowledge Test Questions

Practice Beginner's Permit Knowledge Test

To practice for the beginner's permit test, you may download the free app to your smartphone. Search for the app under "**SC DMV Driver Exam**" with this logo. The practice test offers a series of randomly selected questions. Each question is based on the information found in in this manual.

Sample Knowledge Test Questions

Select the alternative (a, b or c) that **best** answers the question.

1. Alcohol and other impairing drugs
    a. reduce your judgment.
    b. decrease your reaction time.
    c. improve your ability to focus.

2. A yellow dashed line on your side of the roadway only means
    a. passing is prohibited on both sides.
    b. passing is permitted on both sides.
    c. passing is permitted on your side.

3. If you arrive at a four-way intersection controlled by stop signs at the same time as another driver, you should
    a. continue through the intersection.
    b. yield the right-of-way to the driver on your right.
    c. let the driver on your left go first.

4. Which sign warns a divided highway begins?

a.

b.

c.

5. This road signs means
    a. right curve.
    b. curvy road ahead.
    c. sharp curve ahead.

6. Regulatory signs are:
    a. green.
    b. yellow.
    c. white.

7. If a pedestrian is crossing in the middle of the street, not at a crosswalk (also known as jaywalking), even if it is illegal, you
    a. must stop for them.
    b. do not have to stop for them.
    c. should honk your horn at them.

8. Motorcycle operators have the right to
    a. use a complete traffic lane.
    b. share a traffic lane with a vehicle.
    c. use the shoulder of a roadway.

9. When approaching or passing a bicyclist, you should
    a. slow down and allow as much space as possible.
    b. sound your horn to alert your presence.
    c. speed up and quickly pass the bicyclist.

10. When driving at night use your high beams when
    a. fog, rain, or snow is present.
    b. following another vehicle.
    c. there is **no** oncoming traffic approaching.

Correct Answers: 1. a; 2. c; 3. b; 4. a; 5. c; 6. c; 7. a; 8. a; 9. a; 10. c

Made in the USA
Columbia, SC
04 January 2025

51180891R00072